Improving
Your
Study
Skills

Portable Edition

Improving
Your
Study
Skills
Portable Edition

STUDY SMART. STUDY LESS.

Shelley O'Hara

WILEY

Wiley Publishing, Inc.

ISBN-13: 978-0-470-05647-9
ISBN-10: 0-470-05647-9

Manufactured in the United States of America
10 9 8 7 6 5 4 3 2 1
Book design by LeAndra Hosier
Cover design by Jose Almaguer
Page creation by Wiley Publishing, Inc. Composition Services

Table of Contents

8   Writing Papers **127**

Introduction

If you've purchased this book or are thinking about doing so, you're taking a step in the right direction. You may wonder whether you can improve your skills or whether you're stuck the way you are. You may wonder just how much extra effort you need to make to improve your grades. The answer to both is "you can," and this book shows you how.

You *can* improve your grades and skills in all areas. You weren't born with an inability to write or do well in math or any other subject. Yes, some people do have innate abilities, but that doesn't mean you can't do well in these subjects if you put forth the effort.

Improving your study skills doesn't mean spending 24 hours a day, 7 days a week studying. Instead, you can make simple changes to how you approach your schoolwork. You can better manage your time. You can find your best method for approaching assignments. You can learn how to get extra help when needed. This book covers these topics and more.

Whether your current skills are good, mediocre, or poor, you can develop study habits and attitudes that will help you not only in school, but also in your career, relationships, and all of life.

Simple Rules for Success

Becoming a better student, managing your time and organizing your work, prioritizing your assignments, getting the most from a reading assignment or lecture, and quickly handling problems are all ways to improve your success in school. And all of these habits and skills can all be enhanced by following key guidelines:

✓ **Realize that your attitude makes a difference.** If you believe you can do better, you will. Approach all your schoolwork with a positive attitude.

✓ **Do your homework and assignments on time.** One of the main ways students fall behind is simply not doing assignments unless there's a test or quiz. Instead, complete your reading

1

assignments and homework when they're assigned. If you keep up with your daily work, you immediately recognize if there's something you don't understand and can get help with it. Also, doing your homework enables you to practice well in advance of a test or a day when an assignment is due.

✓ **Check your work.** Sloppiness or careless mistakes can make a difference. Checking your work, following instructions exactly, and using proper grammar and spelling show your instructor your commitment to excellence in the big and little areas.

✓ **Realize the importance of reading, note-taking, and writing.** These are skills you'll use in many subjects throughout your education, so it's worth your effort to learn how to get the most from your reading, how to effectively take notes, and how to improve your writing skills. (This book includes chapters on each of these topics.)

✓ **When you have a major assignment, break it down into smaller parts and get started right away.** If you break it down into steps, you won't be overwhelmed. And by not waiting until the last minute, you'll have plenty of time to not only do the work but also check and fine-tune the assignment, as needed.

✓ **Don't wait to study the night before the test.** Instead, have study sessions before the test and use the last night only as a mini-review.

✓ **Ask for help if you need it.** There's nothing wrong with asking for help if you don't understand a topic or are struggling with a concept. You can ask your instructor for help or you can seek help from outside sources.

✓ **Use technology, when possible, to make the work easier.** Technology makes doing research easier and more convenient. You'll find tips throughout the book on how to use technology to your advantage; there's also a entire chapter (Chapter 9) devoted to using technology.

✓ **Know that there's always room for improvement.** Among the best and the worst students, everyone can always do better.

✓ **Have fun.** When you approach your school work with curiosity and creativity, you'll find that it's much more enjoyable. And when you enjoy your work, you're likely to do better.

What This Book Contains

The preceding section gives you a list of the most important and basic ideas for succeeding in school. You can find more details in each of the 10 chapters in the book. Keep in mind that you can choose to start with Chapter 1 and read sequentially through the book, or you can concentrate on only a chapter that deals with a topic on which you need help.

The chapters and a short description of each follow:

Chapter 1, "Making Good Grades," provides the basics of what instructors expect and what you should be prepared to do to improve your study skills (and grades).

Chapter 2, "Getting Organized," gives you some advice on how to best manage your time and your space. Organization is important, because being organized helps you locate what you need (rather than waste time looking for things) and most importantly, helps you make sure you know what assignments are due. You can then plan your time accordingly.

Chapter 3, "Reading," focuses on one of the most important skills you need for learning — reading. In this chapter, you not only see how to best approach a reading assignment but also understand how to spot the most important information in a reading assignment and how to take notes on your reading. The chapter also provides additional tips, if you're struggling with reading.

Chapter 4, "Taking Notes," describes how to take notes from a lecture or reading so that when you're studying for a test, you have good, reliable, relevant notes to use. Many students aren't taught how to take notes, but it's a critical skill. This chapter helps you listen for the main ideas, organize your notes so that it's clear how information is related, and use some shortcuts to simplify note-taking.

Chapter 5, "Studying for Tests," is the first of two chapters on taking tests. This chapter starts by teaching you how to gather information about the test, and then use that information to anticipate what the test will cover and what types of questions are likely to be included. You'll also learn the best and most effective ways to review and prepare for tests by studying from your reading notes, lecture notes, and homework.

Chapter 6, "Taking Tests," explains last-minute preparations for the test as well as how to manage your time and plan your strategies when you are actually taking the text. For instance, in Chapter 6, you discover some tips and strategies for taking certain types of tests, answering certain kinds of questions, and preparing for and taking tests on a variety of subjects or classes (math, literature, and history, for example).

Chapter 7, "Doing Research," tells you what to expect when your instructor assigns a research assignment. You start by reviewing the assignment itself, so you know exactly what the instructor expects and exactly what you need to complete. The chapter also discusses how to select a topic, find resources (from your textbook to the Internet), and include appropriate research that's cited properly.

Chapter 8, "Writing Papers," describes the steps for writing a paper, explains how to avoid the fear of the blank page, details the elements of a successful paper, builds on research skills covered in Chapter 7, and stresses the importance of editing your paper.

Technology can be a big advantage in doing your assignments, from homework to research projects. Chapter 9, "Using Technology," explains various ways you can use technology to simplify studying. More importantly, it also stresses how to keep your work organized on your computer as well as protect your work (by making backups, avoiding viruses, and so on).

Chapter 10, "Getting Extra Help," explains avenues you can explore if you find you need extra help. For example, you may need some help with reading assignments, or you may struggle with writing. The chapter explains the many options you have for extra help, from school resources to outside tutoring.

The book also includes a self-administered test that you can take to pinpoint your strengths and weaknesses. The quiz also points to particular chapters to get help for troublesome study skills.

Now that you know how this book can help you master excellent study skills and habits, you're ready to get started. With effort, your success, confidence, and opportunities will grow.

Test Yourself

One of the ways to improve your study skills is to evaluate your strengths (and weaknesses). Take this quick quiz to see how your skills rate.

Directions: Circle your answer for each question (1 = never, 2 = sometimes, 3 = always), and then total the score for each section. The scoring summary is at the end of the quiz.

Planning Your Classes (Chapter 1)

1. I spend time thinking about what classes I should take based on important factors (versus deciding on a class because it's easy or at a convenient time).

   1   2   3

2. I know the requirements of all the classes I take, including how I will be assessed and what materials I need.

   1   2   3

3. I treat my teacher with respect and feel comfortable asking questions if I don't understand something.

   1   2   3

4. I arrive to my classes on time.

   1   2   3

5. I have a good idea of what my grades are in my classes at all times (not just when I receive midterm grades or other progress reports).

   1   2   3

Organizational and Time Management Skills (Chapter 2)

1. I use folders and notebooks for each of my subjects.

   1   2   3

2. I keep an assignment notebook (or similar list) to keep track of my homework and major assignments.

   1   2   3

3. I have a special study area where I can do my work undisturbed, and I have all the supplies I need handy (without having to get up and search for books or pens or papers).

   1   2   3

4. I turn in my homework assignments on time.

   1   2   3

5. When I have a major assignment, I start working on it well before the deadline rather than the night before.

   1   2   3

Reading (Chapter 3)

1. I preview a reading assignment before starting to read, and I note key elements such as the chapter outline, discussion questions, and illustrations.

   1   2   3

2. I can find the main idea in a paragraph or series of paragraphs.

   1   2   3

3. I take notes on my reading assignments, and these notes help me later when I have to study for a test or write a paper.

   1   2   3

4. I have a good sense of the important facts, concepts, or ideas in a reading assignment.

    1   2   3

5. I allow plenty of time to do my reading assignments instead of waiting until the last minute.

    1   2   3

Taking Notes (Chapter 4)

1. I know how to listen for the important information in a lecture and how to effectively record that information in my notes.

    1   2   3

2. I look for certain clues (such as charts or information that is repeated more than once) when I take notes.

    1   2   3

3. I use some shorthand method (such as using abbreviations) to help me quickly write my notes.

    1   2   3

4. I review my notes and organize them, looking for gaps and filling in any missing information.

    1   2   3

5. When I study for a test that's based on notes (from a lecture or reading), I find that my notes help me be well-prepared; that is, my notes are relevant and useful study guides.

    1   2   3

Studying for Tests (Chapter 5)

1. When a test date approaches, I know exactly what to expect — what types of questions, what's covered, when the test is scheduled, and so on.

    1   2   3

2. I use my experience from past tests and from my reading to anticipate the questions I think are likely to be on the test.

   1   2   3

3. I plan my study time so that I have plenty of time to review (instead of cramming at the last minute).

   1   2   3

4. For subjects (like math) that involve problem-solving, I practice sample problems, especially those that I struggle with.

   1   2   3

5. I've done my reading, homework, and in-class assignments on time so I don't have any make-up reading or work to do to study for a test.

   1   2   3

Taking Tests (Chapter 6)

1. I have a positive attitude about tests, and even if I have a negative attitude, I know that with work and effort, I can change how I view taking tests.

   1   2   3

2. When I receive the test, I skim through and note the types of questions. I also use this quick read-through to plan and budget my time for each section of the test.

   1   2   3

3. I always leave enough time to go back over the test and check my answers.

   1   2   3

4. When answering an essay question, I think about what I want to say, and then jot down a quick list or outline, so that I plan my response (instead of just writing).

   1   2   3

5. When the teacher returns the test, I review the results, noting where I did well and where I need to improve.

   1   2   3

Doing Research (Chapter 7)

1. When given a research assignment, I make sure I understand all the requirements of the assignment.

   1   2   3

2. I select a topic that not only meets the requirements of the assignment but also is interesting and relevant to the subject.

   1   2   3

3. I know how to use the resources at my school and my local library; if I don't, I ask for help.

   1   2   3

4. I know how to use the Internet to do research, and I also evaluate the source of the information to be sure it's credible.

   1   2   3

5. I understand when I need to cite information I include in a paper (to avoid plagiarism), and I know the proper format for including a Works Cited list.

   1   2   3

Writing Papers (Chapter 8)

1. When I write a paper, I spend time thinking about the topic and the point I want to make, because I know these elements are key to a successful paper.

   1   2   3

2. I know strategies for brainstorming topic ideas as well as ways to find appropriate resources for my paper.

   1   2   3

3. I know different methods and strategies for organizing my paper.

    1   2   3

4. I leave enough time when working on a paper for editing and revising.

    1   2   3

5. I check my paper for grammatical or spelling errors. I also proofread (versus relying on my word processing program to find errors).

    1   2   3

Using Technology (Chapter 9)

1. I put the technology I have available to use in many different ways (writing, communicating, researching, and so on).

    1   2   3

2. I either have access to a computer at home, or I have alternative places to gain access (school, local library, and so on).

    1   2   3

3. When I'm working on any type of document (paper, presentation, worksheet), I save — and save often.

    1   2   3

4. I keep my work organized on the computer by setting up and using folders and also by using descriptive file names.

    1   2   3

5. I know the basics of searching for information on the Internet.

    1   2   3

Getting Extra Help (Chapter 10)

1. I know the warning signs (a drop in grades or a lack of interest) that may indicate I need some extra help.

    1   2   3

2. When I realize I have a problem, I spend time trying to identify the cause (not doing the work, not listening to the teacher, not understanding the material, and so on).

    1   2   3

3. I know that there's nothing wrong with getting extra help and that even good students get help.

    1   2   3

4. I know what resources are available at my school for extra help.

    1   2   3

5. If the school doesn't have the resources I need, I try to seek outside help by using a tutor, a form of self-study (like a workbook), or some other method.

    1   2   3

Scoring

Total your scores for each section, and then use the following scale to see how you rate in that particular study skill area.

11–15	You have good to excellent skills in this area.
6–10	You are average and could work on improving your skills in this area.
5 or below	You need to put more emphasis on improving your skills in this area.

This book is designed to build and improve all the study skills. The following chart tells you which chapters can help with various skills. Strive to put the suggestions into effect; doing so is likely to improve your study skills and grades.

Planning	Chapter 1
Time Management and Organizational Skills	Chapter 2
Reading	Chapter 3
Taking Notes	Chapter 4
Studying for Tests	Chapter 5
Taking Tests	Chapter 6
Doing Research	Chapter 7
Writing Papers	Chapter 8
Using Technology	Chapter 9
Getting Extra Help	Chapter 10

Making Good Grades

> *I am still learning.*
>
> —Michelangelo

You may feel pressure from your parents or instructors to make good grades, but to achieve real success, you have to want to do well yourself. The drive and goals and desire have to come from you. Although your instructors, parents, siblings, and friends can encourage you, the responsibility is yours to decide to do your best. You must be willing to dedicate the time and effort needed to succeed in school. No one can do that for you.

Doing your best without any guidance is difficult. That's the purpose of this book: to help you make effective use of your time, study better, prepare for class, know and meet the expectations of your instructor, and more.

This chapter discusses some basic factors or attitudes you need to master, including how to plan your schedule, prepare for class, know the course requirements, and do the required work.

Planning Your Schedule

In some schools, you get to choose the classes you take. If you don't get to choose, you can skip this section, but do pay attention to Chapter 2, which covers how to manage your time (homework time, sports activities, and so on). If you do get to select your classes, read this section for advice on how to choose classes suited for both your educational requirements as well as your interests. If you pick classes of special interest to you, you are more likely to *want* to do the work, and your grades may reflect your interest.

WHAT CLASSES DO YOU HAVE TO TAKE?

You need to determine which classes are required for you to pass to the next grade (or to graduate, depending on where you are in your school career). Requirements are usually set by the state and local government, school district, or college. Required courses may vary from state to state and even school to school. For example, your school may require you to take a certain number of foreign language classes. Some private schools even require you to master a musical instrument, participate in drama or sports, and/or engage in volunteer work before you can graduate.

Your school should provide a list of courses that are required for your grade level. You can also check with your guidance counselor or advisor to help plan your courses.

WHAT CLASSES ARE AVAILABLE?

Next you need to determine which courses are offered at your school and at what times. The school may publish a course guide with a short description of the class and its meeting time and instructor. You can use this to get a good idea of the various classes offered.

Ask Classmates

Although you can get class information from your school Web site or course list, this information usually gives you only the bare minimum. Go, instead, to your best resource: students who have taken that course. These students can tell you how much work is involved, whether the instructor presents the information in an engaging way (or is a bore), and other factors that can help you select your classes.

Think Ahead

If you're in high school and planning to go to college, keep in mind that college admissions offices look closely at the courses you take. Therefore, don't take only easy electives. In addition, try to build your electives around a theme or set of skills instead of taking classes randomly.

If your school has a Web site, it may also list available classes along with a description, meeting time(s), and the instructor that teaches that class. You can use these resources to select courses of interest to you.

WHAT CLASSES DO YOU WANT TO TAKE?

After you list the classes you need to take, you can then decide how many elective courses you can take. *Elective courses* are courses that aren't required but that still count toward your diploma or degree requirements. For example, you may want to take a drawing class if you're interested in art. If you like drama and your school offers drama classes, you can sign up for one of these courses. You can use the list of available classes at your school to select your elective classes.

If you're an honor student, you may seek out elective classes that help you prepare for college. For example, perhaps your school requires only two science courses, but your main interest is in science. In this case, you may want to take additional science courses. The same goes for math courses or other tough classes that students usually don't think of as fun electives.

WHEN IS THE CLASS AND WHAT ARE THE REQUIREMENTS?

Two factors to consider when choosing classes are the time the course is offered and the requirements of the class. Obviously, you can't schedule two classes at the same time on the same day, so you may need to make some alternative plans if desired classes clash.

Best Time of Day

While you won't always be able to schedule your classes around the hours you prefer, do take into consideration when you're at your best. If you're a morning person, you may prefer scheduling your hardest morning classes. If you have trouble waking up and don't feel alert until mid-morning, schedule your more difficult classes for later in the day, if possible.

Also, take into consideration the requirements of the class. What types of assessments are used? Tests? Papers? Projects? How much homework is typical for that class? You don't want to overload your class schedule; instead, you want to be able to devote the necessary time needed for each class. If you think your plans are too ambitious, consider reworking your schedule. You're better off doing well in all your classes (a mix of harder and easier ones) than taking only hard classes and having problems in one (or more) of them. On the flip side, don't load up on all easy classes, either. Too many easy classes won't prepare you for the challenges ahead. Strive for a balance.

Note, too, that some courses require labs in addition to the regular class time. For example, most science courses require you to do lab work *and* attend the lecture classes.

Another factor to consider is that some courses have *prerequisites* — that is, other courses you must take and pass before you can be admitted into a particular course. Course prerequisites should be listed in the course schedule.

Finally, keep in mind any extracurricular activities that you participate in. Chapter 2 goes into more detail about managing your time, but think about your hobbies and extracurriculars when selecting your classes and planning your course schedule.

Knowing What Your Instructor Expects

When your classes begin and you are introduced to your instructor, you should make sure you know what the expectations are for the class. The instructor should provide detailed guidelines about the expectations for the class. Usually, these are written and included as a handout, and they may also be posted on a school Web site. If you aren't provided with written guidelines, be sure to take notes and ask questions if there are assignments or rules you don't understand. Knowing what's expected of you helps you set goals for what you want to accomplish. Also, the expectations of the class (and how well you meet them) are what determine your grade in the class. To do well, you need to make sure you meet (and exceed) the requirements and expectations of that class.

In general, your instructor will usually provide you with the following information:

✓ **Assessments:** How are grades determined? By tests? Papers? A combination of factors? The grading criteria should be explicitly covered at the beginning of class so that you know exactly what you need to do to get a good grade in that class. Spelling out the grading methods also prevents the instructor from assigning grades arbitrarily.

✓ **Class policies:** Your instructor should spell out the attendance policy. If you miss class, does it affect your grade? How should you notify the instructor if you're going to miss a class? What about late assignments? Is a late assignment penalized? If so, in what way?

✓ **Contact methods:** Your instructor should tell you how he or she prefers to be contacted. For example, if you have an e-mail system at your school, can you e-mail your instructor if you're going to be absent? Can you get assignments you missed via e-mail?

✓ **Class participation:** Does the instructor expect you to be actively involved in discussion? Does the course use peer

Not Sure How Grades Are Determined?

Your instructor should outline at the very start of a class how grades are determined. In college and high school classes, you usually get a syllabus that outlines the course topics, assignments, deadlines, and other important information. In grade-school classes, the instructor may orally explain the grading procedure. If you aren't given this information or aren't sure how grades are determined, ask your instructor. You want to know beforehand rather than after the class has ended how your class performance will be assessed.

evaluation (for example, in reading and making suggestions on rough drafts of papers)? Does part of your grade consist of class participation? Are you penalized if you don't participate?

✓ **Questions:** Usually, you raise your hand and wait to be called on, but your instructor may have other preferences on how to participate or ask questions.

Instructors have difficult jobs, and they usually teach because they enjoy it. What makes them happy is to see you progress and succeed. No matter what your skill level, they want to see you trying your hardest. They want to make you feel excited about learning and show this excitement. Knowing what the instructor hopes to achieve overall can help you better understand the instructor's motives and expectations.

A GOOD STUDENT . . .

Instructors often spell out the qualities or expectations for a good student. If not, the following list gives you some idea of what the instructor ideally expects from you:

✓ Treat the instructor with respect and courtesy. Be polite.

✓ Be honest. Rather than lie about being late or not having an assignment, tell the truth (and accept the consequences). The instructor will respect you more if you tell the truth rather than make up some obvious lie.

✓ Come to class on time.

✓ Do the assignments for class and meet all deadlines for projects. Be prepared for tests.

✓ If you have to miss a class, let the instructor know ahead of time, if possible. Also, arrange to get the homework so that you aren't behind when you return.

✓ Wait to be called on if you have a question.

✓ Participate in class discussions and ask questions. Doing so shows the instructor that you're paying attention and are actively applying the information.

✓ Ask for extra help after or before class (or at some other prearranged time) if you're struggling with a concept or project. Doing so shows the instructor you're aware that you aren't doing as well as you want, that you need help, and that you're taking responsibility by asking for help.

A Problem Student . . .

Most good instructors focus on positive behaviors and don't outline the qualities of a problem student. Still, you can generally expect instructors to find the following classroom actions unacceptable:

✓ Talking when someone else is talking, whether that's the instructor or another classmate.

✓ Blurting out a question or answer without being called on.

✓ Coming late to class.

✓ Being unprepared for class.

✓ Making up excuses or lying about being late or not having work done.

✓ Distracting other classmates from their work.

✓ Bullying, demeaning, threatening, or harassing another student or the instructor.

✓ Bringing distractions (magazines, CD or MP3 players, toys, and so on) to class. This may also include food, drinks, and even chewing gum.

✓ Cheating on a paper, homework assignment, test, quiz, or other class work. (See the "Doing Your Work" section for more on the types of assignments that may be required for your class.)

Preparing for Class

Instructors expect you to come to class prepared. The better prepared you are, the more you'll get from the class. This means that you should:

✓ **Complete any homework assignments.**

✓ **Read any reading assignments** (and take notes on them).

✓ **Review your lecture notes** from the preceding class so that you remember what has been covered and where you are in the discussion of the topic.

In your reading or review of lecture notes, jot down any questions you have or concepts you don't understand. If you think the class will benefit from asking the question in class, do so. (Other students may have the same questions but don't want to say anything.) If the question is personal or limited and wouldn't likely be of interest to the class, talk to the instructor before or after class or during his or her office hours.

✓ **Participate in class discussions.** Not only does this show your instructor that you're actively engaged in the course but it also gives you a chance to explore related information, express your opinion, and connect ideas to other topics you know about.

Doing Your Work

Your instructor should outline the requirements of the class at the beginning of the class (as well as remind you throughout the semester about upcoming tests or papers). Good students do their work, following the instructions given by the instructor. They also turn in their work on time. Part of doing well in school boils down to simply this: your work!

Later chapters talk in more detail about how to take good notes (Chapter 4), study for tests (Chapters 5 and 6), write effective papers (Chapter 8), and so on. The following is a quick summary of the types of work you can expect to do for your classes:

✓ **Homework or daily assignments:** Your instructor may give you homework or assignments that you're expected to complete within a short time span (for example, for the next class). Usually, these help you practice a concept or skill and also help the instructor see whether anyone in the class is struggling with the concepts. For example, in a math class, you can expect to have homework just about every night; these assignments help you solve sample problems so that when you're given similar problems on the test, you have had practice (and feedback) on your progress.

✓ **Reading assignments:** For most classes, you'll be expected to read. In history, for example, you may read a chapter about the Great Depression or other period in history. In a literature class, you may read a novel or play. You may think that you can skip the reading until the actual test or paper due date, but that's not a good strategy. First, the instructor usually lectures on content from reading assignments. If you've

Easy Points!

Often, quizzes and homework assignments — combined together — make up a good portion of your final grade. While they may not be weighted as heavy as a midterm or final exam, they can have an impact. Use these short and relatively simple assessments to boost your grade rather than drag it down.

done the reading, you can more easily follow along. Second, trying to read an entire novel (or several chapters) before a test doesn't allow you enough time to fully comprehend the information and study the main themes and concepts.

Chapter 4 covers taking notes on both lectures and reading assignments in more detail and also stresses the importance of doing your reading assignments before class.

✓ **Quizzes:** You may have *pop* (unannounced) quizzes or scheduled quizzes. Both help you and your instructor determine how well you understand the material you're learning about. For example, if you get 7 out of 10 questions wrong on a quiz, this raises a flag that you need to do your reading, review your notes, and study more.

✓ **Tests:** In many courses, you take tests to assess your understanding of the material. You may take a test at the end of each lesson. Or you may take a test midway through the semester, and then another test at the end. Your instructor should explain to you what to expect on a test (which types of questions, which book chapters are covered, and so on). You find out more about preparing for tests in Chapter 5.

✓ **Papers:** Some courses require you to complete a paper or research project as part of the course grade. Usually, the instructor gives you precise details about what's expected (length of the paper, appropriate topics, sources to use, and so on). You discover more about researching in Chapter 7 and writing papers in Chapter 9.

✓ **Other assessments:** The preceding bullets cover the most common assessment types, but your course may require other types. For example, in a speech class, you may be required to give a speech or presentation. In a science class, you usually have to demonstrate competence in lab procedures, such as dissecting a frog or identifying the internal organs of an earthworm. For an art class, you may create an art project.

2

Getting Organized

“ *Yesterday is history. Tomorrow is a
mystery. And today? Today is a gift.
That's why we call it the present.* ”

—Babatunde Olatunji

One of the easiest ways to waste time is to be disorganized. If you
can't find your assignment or don't know where the book you need
is, you'll spend a lot of time looking around (and getting distracted). Your time is valuable. That's why it's key that you not only
organize your space so that you can find what you need, but also
manage your time so that you know what needs to be done when.

This chapter focuses on organization: your work space, your
supplies, your time, and your extracurricular activities.

Organizing Your Study Space

The first thing to consider is finding a dedicated space to study
and keep your supplies at home or in your dorm. You may have a
desk in your room or in another part of the house, like in a family
room or home office. Dedicate this spot to studying and keep it
free from distractions.

Yes, there'll be times when you'll need to work in other places.
For example, if you're working on an art project, you might work
in the kitchen or in the garage. If you're reading, consider reading

in your bedroom. Regardless of where you choose, it's important to have one main space for your school work.

Helpful Items in a Good Study Space

You can go hog wild and find all kinds of furniture and equipment to organize your workspace, but you don't need each and every organizational gadget out there. You just need some basic pieces. You can then consider some of the extra stuff.

A good study space should have the following:

✓ **A work space (either a desk or table where you can write or draw or solve math problems):** The space should have enough room for you to spread out your work so that you can keep the tools you need (paper, books, pen, protractor, calculator, and so on) at your fingertips.

✓ **A good chair:** You want something that's comfortable and supports you with good posture. A bean bag chair, for example, isn't a good study chair. Instead, use an adjustable office chair or other chair that's the right height for your workspace.

✓ **A place for books:** You need a place to store the books you use frequently, such as a dictionary, thesaurus, or atlas. Keep your school books close by so that you don't have to get up and find your backpack when you're working on your homework. Use a small bookcase, desk drawers, or shelves on the wall.

✓ **Good lighting:** You need adequate lighting for you to see your work clearly. Sometimes, an overhead light is not enough, so consider a desk lamp or a floor lamp that shines light where you need it.

✓ **Outlets:** If you use a computer to do your homework or to study, you need access to outlets in which to plug in the computer, even if it's a laptop. You'll also need to plug in your desk lamp and any other equipment that requires electricity.

> ## Put Stuff Back!
>
> If you work on an assignment in another area, put your sup-
> plies back where you normally keep them. This saves you from
> searching the house for the colored pencils you need to
> finish a social studies project that are not in their desig-
> nated spot.

✓ **Writing tools and other supplies:** You might store your pens,
  pencils, rulers, protractors, and so on in a desk drawer or in
  a holder on your desk. Know what tools you need to complete your homework and make sure they're handy.

In addition, your study space may include other elements that
help you organize your work. Consider buying a filing cabinet to
keep all your files organized into folders. Or you might create
labeled boxes (a la Martha Stewart) to keep your supplies organized and looking neat and chic.

A bulletin board is a great addition. You can post reminders of
upcoming assignments, including a calendar of key assignment
dates. As another alternative, you may have a large desk calendar
that you use to write down assignments and test dates. The "Managing Your Time" section goes into more detail about managing
your schedule using tools like these.

AVOIDING DISTRACTIONS

Your study area should *not* include distractions. These include TVs,
game systems (PlayStation, Xboxes, Gameboys, and so on), and
music (stereos, iPods, Walkmans, or other portable players). You
may think that you can read or study with MTV on in the background, but chances are, you'll get distracted. Either place your
study area away from your entertainment area or make sure all of
this equipment is off and stays off.

Also, don't answer your phone while you're studying unless it's important. In fact, you might turn off your cellphone if you get a lot of calls. Unless an important call comes through, let the answering machine or voice mail pick up or tell the person you'll call back. It's too easy to get involved in a conversation and forget about your homework.

Finally, if you work on a computer, don't let e-mail — and especially Instant Messaging — distract you from doing your work. You can send a quick message to your online buddies saying that you're busy and will connect with them later. Note that this takes discipline, but guarding your time and space ensures you have the time you need.

ORGANIZING YOUR SPACE AT SCHOOL

Even though you may have a desk and some type of storage space for your books and supplies at school, you should still keep these items organized. Put stuff back so that you know where to find it. Keep your locker and desk clean (recycle any papers you don't need, for example). Use any assignment tools provided by your school, such as an assignment board or assignment notebook.

Keeping Track of Your Work

You have the space to do your work, now you have to consider how to keep the work itself organized. Looking through a stack of papers to find the one you need for an assignment wastes time. Forgetting to bring home a paper or book you need can hurt your grade on that assignment (or annoy your parents or roommates if you have to go back to school to get the assignment). The following sections describe some strategies for keeping your assignments, books, notes, and other information organized.

Usually, at the beginning of school, you get a list of school supplies and most often, this list includes the number of notebooks and folders you need. You'll probably need one notebook for each subject, sometimes two. Label your notebooks and use the right notebook for the right class. If you have to take notes for a

Keep Your Parents Informed

One of the biggest complaints from parents is that they are not always aware of things going on at school. This is often because instructors send handouts or flyers home with the student, but the student may not be relaying that information in a timely fashion (or not at all).

As a grade-school or high-school student, make sure you share with your parents not only communication about school events but also your graded tests and homework. Designate a special folder and place all handouts in this folder. You can get a lot of paper — tryouts for basketball, music program schedules, extracurricular activities, and so on — so stay on top of these papers *before* you get overwhelmed and disorganized.

subject, do so neatly so that you can read them. (Chapter 4 covers taking notes in more detail.)

You also may keep papers related to each subject in a special folder. To start, label your folders, and when you get a handout, put it in the correct folder. This helps you find that paper when you need it. Periodically clean out your folders and get rid of old papers.

For example, suppose you're doing a social studies project on Italy and have collected pictures and information from books and the Internet. Save all this information in a folder so that you can quickly find it when you need it.

Find a place at home to also store important papers that you want to save (for example, test scores or major assignments). You might purchase a storage box and save some of your favorite assignments. You may also want to save important graded assignments until after you receive your report card in case there are any discrepancies in the grades. You can save this information in some type of filing system: boxes, a filing cabinet, or some other means.

If you use a computer, keep your information organized on that as well. Chapter 9 provides information on how to set up folders to store your work, keep a list of important Web sites, and back up your work for safekeeping.

Managing Your Time

The best students are those who use their time effectively. The first part of this chapter shows you some ways that organization can help you avoid distractions and save time so that you can easily find and access what you need when you study or work on an assignment. In addition to these helpful organizational strategies, you need to plan and maintain your schedule, not only of class times and assignments, but also for fun and extracurricular activities.

While it may seem like a drag to write down all the things you have to do, it's actually very freeing. When you've recorded the key dates (and steps for completing an assignment), you don't have to worry about your time as much because you have a plan. You don't have to worry about what's due when and what you've forgotten, because you have it recorded. And when you do have free time, you'll enjoy it, because you won't have to worry about what you should be doing. Changing your attitude about time management may be the biggest hurdle, but after you've mastered this skill, you'll find it has big rewards.

WAYS TO RECORD YOUR SCHEDULE

To manage your time, you need both due dates and a way to record that information. You may want to use one or several methods for tracking and managing your schedule. Consider some of the following:

✓ **Assignment book:** It's a good idea to carry an assignment book or calendar book with room to write down assignments. This should fit in your backpack, so that you can record dates for assignments as the instructor tells you or from handouts. This is your traveling time management tool, and you want to have it with you in each class.

✓ **Daily to-do lists:** This is covered in detail in the "Making a To-Do List" section.

✓ **Desk or wall calendar:** In addition to an assignment book that keeps track of daily homework and upcoming assignments, you may want a master calendar that you place on your desk or hang on a wall. You may choose to record only big assignments and tests as well as school events, such as days off, athletic events, and dances. If you play a sport, you may record your practice times and games on this big calendar as well.

✓ **PDA (personal digital assistant):** Some students choose to use a PDA, which is a combination of tools, including a contact manager and a scheduler. While you may note some information in these schedulers, I don't recommend using one as your sole time-management tool, because for many people, printed information stands out better than information on a screen, but some PDAs do allow you to print your schedule. Also, it's easy to lose a PDA or to lose data if you don't back up the information (see Chapter 9). So it's not the most reliable method, although some people prefer this time-management tool and do make it work.

PLANNING CLASS TIME

Now that you know the various ways you can track all the things you need to do, places you need to go, and people you need to meet, start thinking about exactly where you need to be, what you need to do, and whom you need to meet. Start by blocking out your class schedule. For each class, block out the class time and record any key dates for major assignments. Sometimes, the instructor will include a syllabus with key dates (see Chapter 1). Other times, tests and assignment dates are given throughout the course. Regardless, note these in your daily assignment book as well as your big overview calendar so that these dates stand out.

Making a To-Do List

A good way to keep track of your daily work, especially if you don't keep an assignment notebook or if you don't have room on your calendar, is to create a to-do list. On this list, write all the tasks you need to accomplish, both school-related and personal tasks. After you've written the list, prioritize the items. For example, studying for a final in world history is more important than going shopping for a new belt. You can assign letters (A=most important, B=important, C=somewhat important), numbers, or some other method to indicate which tasks you need to complete.

If you do keep a to-do list, crossing off all that you've accomplished can feel great. For tasks you didn't get to, move them to the next day's list (or evaluate them by asking yourself whether they really need to be done).

Planning Study Time

In addition to class time and assignments and tests, include in your schedule study time for each class. Rather than studying when you can, build studying time into your schedule. Doing so ensures you have time to do that class's homework, reading, and preparing for major assignments.

It's difficult to know how much time per class per week you need to block out, because the amount can vary. For example, some weeks, your workload may be light; others, you may be swamped.

What to Include

Keep your to-do list streamlined by not including stuff that you do everyday. I once had a friend whose to-do list read like this: get out of bed, brush teeth, comb hair, put on makeup, eat breakfast, and so on. You get the idea. She'd have about 100 things on her list, which not only made her feel overwhelmed but also made her lose focus on what was really important on her list.

Ask Your Instructor

Your instructor is a good resource for how much out-of-class study time is expected. Ask the instructor how much time he or she expects you to devote to studying outside class.

At the start of each week, think about what you'll be doing in class, and then try to gauge your time allotment accordingly.

Also, keep in mind your attention span. You might want to block out four hours to study for a class or prepare for a project, but that's a big chunk of time. Be realistic about how much time you can really sit down and work on something. Finally, build in break times so that you can walk away, eat a snack, watch a bit of TV, rejuvenate your brain, and then return to your studies.

PLANNING TIME FOR BIG ASSIGNMENTS

In many classes, you'll have major assignments — big tests or projects. Instead of noting the deadline on your schedule, make a plan of what you need to do to complete the assignment or study for the test, and then include this time in your schedule.

For example, if you have a science project, you might break it down into these steps:

1. Research possible topics and decide on a topic.

2. Research information on topic at your school, at the library, on the Internet, or by using other resources.

3. Plan and then perform any tests to prove/disprove your theory.

4. Create any visuals.

5. Write and arrange the information about the topic, the results of your tests, and your conclusions.

6. Plan and create the final project (for example, on three-panel pasteboard).

Best Time to Study?

Figure out the time that's best for you to study — that is, when you find it easy to concentrate and are relaxed and can retain information. Whenever possible, schedule your study time during these peak thinking times.

The trick is to include these steps into your schedule so that you aren't left with the whole science project to complete the night before it's due.

The same is true for reading assignments, including books on your various school subjects (social studies, history, and so on), as well as any literature reading. Make a plan for what chapters you'll have read by what date so that when the test date comes, you'll have read the material and can focus on studying (rather than trying to read *and* study at the last minute). For example, using this method, you may have to read two chapters a week, which is much more manageable than thinking about reading a 300-page book.

Participating in Extracurricular Activities

School isn't all about studying and tests; it's also about making friends and having fun. Some of the best learning experiences come from participating in extracurricular activities. Activities foster community among your schoolmates, help build leadership, enable you to express yourself in different ways, and more. When planning your schedule, make time for any extracurricular activities.

Depending on your school, these activities can range from student government to sports teams (football, baseball, basketball, soccer, tennis, kickball, volleyball, and more). You may have a chess club or an academic team that competes in academic meets such as the Academic Olympics or Brain Game. You may have a drama club that puts on plays. Or you may sing in the choir or play a musical instrument in the band.

When you are making your schedule, include any practice or meeting times as well as any key dates (such as games or recitals). Doing so ensures that you don't forget these activities and commitments. Also, you can make sure you coordinate any school work with extracurricular activity. For instance, suppose that you are in a play and practices are scheduled during midterms. You need to make sure that you can do both (with the emphasis on your studying).

Too Much?

Sometimes, extracurricular events can get to be too much, and your life may feel like it's overscheduled and you have no time for fun or relaxing. If so, talk to your parents, instructors, and those who lead the activities to help you make good decisions. Perhaps you should cut back so that you have more free time. If your grades are suffering because you have football practice four nights a week, you may have to cut back on the sports and focus on your grades. But it doesn't have to be an all-or-nothing situation. Look for ways to compromise so that you can stay involved, yet still have free time and time to do your school work.

Reading

*The love of learning, the sequestered
nooks, And the sweet serenity of books.*

—Henry Wadsworth Longfellow

One of the most important skills for learning is reading. In fact, most of your class work will be based on reading assignments. You'll read to learn about new information and ideas, including studies, articles, reports, and so on. You'll read to prepare for tests or to write papers. You'll read histories, details of science experiments, myths about different cultures, concepts about math, methods to remain healthy, descriptions of different types of music, and more. In addition to the reading for school, you'll probably also read for fun.

This chapter covers how to get the most from your reading assignments and also includes strategies for making reading easier.

Having a Plan for Reading Assignments

When faced with a reading assignment, it can seem overwhelming. You may start by counting the pages, and then sigh and wish it were already done. To overcome reading aversion, start with a plan: Figure out the purpose of the reading assignment, look at the source of the assignment, and keep the deadline in mind. When you have a plan, you know what you need to accomplish and how to best do so. That's the first part of handling reading assignments and is the focus of the three following sections.

WHAT'S THE PURPOSE?

The first question to ask is what is the purpose for your reading? The purpose is the "why" of your reading plan. You or your instructor determines the purpose of the reading. For example, your instructor may tell you to read a chapter because the material will be covered on a test. Or you may read an article to do research for a paper. Knowing the reason you're reading can help you find a focus.

Any of the following are possible purposes for reading:

✓ **Studying for a test:** Aha! That's probably the reason you think is most important for doing your reading, but you're wrong. Yes, you need to read to learn — and then test — your knowledge, but that's not the primary purpose for reading (or shouldn't be!).

✓ **Reading to comprehend an idea:** The main purpose in reading is to understand an idea or concept. Keep that always in mind as you read. What is the main idea? What are you learning (reading) about?

✓ **Connecting ideas together:** All reading tells a story, and when you read, you not only need to understand the individual parts of the story but also see how that part connects to other parts. A good portion of learning is simply seeing how things are interconnected. For example, how did Britain's rule of the U.S. colonies ignite the American Revolution?

✓ **Learning more:** Sometimes, you read an overview of a topic or concept to get the big picture. Other times, you go into more depth and learn about a specific idea or concept. You may do this as part of your lesson or do it on your own. For example, you may read about the solar system, and then become interested in space travel or astronomy and pursue those topics on your own.

✓ **Reading to appreciate literature:** For many subjects, your reading assignments will be non-fiction. For other classes, you may read fiction, such as novels, poetry, or plays. (See

Problem Reader?

If you're a slow reader or have been diagnosed with a reading disability, don't despair. You can improve your reading abilities. Consult with a reading specialist at your school or work with a reading tutor.

the "Reading Literature" section later in this chapter.) You may associate this type of reading only with literature or English classes, but often, reading literature is helpful for social studies (to learn about the myths of other cultures, for example), history (to see how events of the time were portrayed in fiction), and other subjects.

✓ **Reading for pleasure:** Many students love reading for their own personal pleasure. You may also love to read, and you may like a particular genre (science fiction, horror, romance, and so on) or a wide variety of styles and types of writing.

WHAT'S THE RESOURCE?

In addition to determining the purpose of the reading assignment, consider the resource. Is it from a textbook? Novel? Workbook? Handout? Other resource, such as an Internet article? The resource is the "what" of your reading plan.

The resource is important because first you must make sure you have access to it. You need to take your textbook home or make sure you have the appropriate handouts. Sometimes, you may need to go to a library (your school or your local one) to do a reading. Or you may need to use the Internet. Regardless, make sure the materials are available.

Also, you need to know the rules for working from that resource. Is the reading your textbook? If so, can you highlight in it and write in the margins? Or do you need to take notes in a separate notebook?

WHEN IS THE READING DUE?

Another factor when completing a reading assignment is doing the reading on time, as scheduled by your instructor. One of the biggest mistakes students make is to put off reading assignments until right before a test or paper. Then they try to cram a lot of reading into a little time, leaving little time for absorbing and making sense of the information.

One of the best ways to do well in school is simple: Do your work when it's assigned. If you're supposed to read Chapters 1 and 2 by a certain date, read Chapters 1 and 2 by that date. Stay up-to-date on your reading assignments! Keeping up on your reading will make it much easier not only to study and prepare for tests and papers but also to actively participate in class.

When planning your reading, look at the length or number of pages you need to read. The length helps you gauge the amount of time you need to read the assignment. (Preview the entire reading and note key elements that help you tie parts together; this is covered later in "Getting the Most from Reading Assignments.")

In addition to looking at the length, think about the difficulty of the reading or the level of reading skill needed. Is the reading dense and packed with information? Or is it a bulleted list of key ideas? The difficulty, like the length, helps you determine how much time and effort you need to devote to the reading assignment.

Reading Long Assignments

If you have a long reading assignment, you may want to break it into shorter reading sessions. For example, if you have a 30-page reading assignment, you may break it into 3 sessions of 10 pages each (or 2 of 15 pages each). Doing so helps you concentrate on the material and not get overwhelmed by the length or complexity of the assignment. Reading 10 to 15 pages is reasonable. Faced with a reasonable assignment, you're more likely to complete that assignment.

Time for Review

When planning the amount of time for the reading, make sure you have time not just for reading but also for taking notes and creating any other materials (an outline or flashcards, for example).

Getting the Most from Reading Assignments

Reading is important, and what many students fail to realize is that you can improve your reading skills. Doing so pays big rewards, because better reading will improve your performance in just about every subject. All readers — not just those that don't like to read or aren't good readers — should look for ways to develop their reading skills. There is always room for improvement. This section includes some key ways to make reading easier and more effective for you.

Many of your readings will be from a textbook, but you may also have reading assignments that consist of articles, Web site information, newspaper stories, and other non-literature selections. The following sections discuss some strategies for approaching reading assignments from a textbook or similar source. See the "Reading Literature" section later in this chapter for strategies for approaching literary reading.

PREVIEWING THE READING

Before you begin reading, take some time to quickly look at the material and note what type of information the reading contains, how it's organized, whether it includes illustrations, and any other details.

A textbook usually provides several layers of meaning and is organized to help you make sense of the information. Usually, the textbook designer and author(s) have created special features to help facilitate learning. (Similarly, this book includes sidebars as extra information you can apply.) Likewise, an article usually has a title and may also include a subtitle, section headings, and illustrations.

When you preview the reading, do the following:

✓ **Skim through the pages.** The length should give you some idea of how much time you need to read the selection. Also, as you skim, note the different types of information. Are there figures? Illustrations? Margin notes? Review questions? Note the difficulty of the reading assignment.

✓ **In a textbook, look at the Table of Contents to get a sense of what you're reading about.** When looking at the Table of Contents, also note how the information is organized, so that you have a sense of how the information is related. Most commonly, writers follow an outline with major headings, and then include minor headings within the major headings. (In more complex books, you may find several layers of headings within sections.) Use this structure to keep in mind an overview of the information, to see how ideas are related, and to develop an outline for your reading notes.

✓ **Read the introduction.** The introduction usually gives you a snapshot or overview of the chapter or article. Also, some textbook chapters list objectives or topics so that you can see in a quick-list format what subjects are covered and what you're expected to be able to do after completing the chapter or lesson.

Parts of Chapter

Even if you're reading only part of a chapter, still read the introduction to the chapter and look through the entire Table of Contents for that chapter. Doing so can help you place into context the specific selection you're reading.

What Do You Already Know?

When previewing a reading assignment, think about what you already know about the subject. Think about how the information you're about to read relates to what you already know. If you're meticulous, you can even take notes on or sketch out the general concepts you already know about the subject. You then fill in new information as you read.

✓ **Note any words or phrases that are in bold or italics.** These are usually terms or concepts that are defined and are usually important to the information within that paragraph.

✓ **Look at each illustration and read the caption.** The old saying, "A picture is worth a thousand words" is true. Think, for example, about trying to describe the solar system in words versus showing a graphic illustration of the planets and their orbits.

Illustrations can be maps, charts, drawings, photographs, and other visual elements. When looking at each illustration, ask yourself what value it adds. Does the illustration just add some extra information? Or is the illustration critical to understanding the subject? Usually, the illustration has a purpose, but sometimes, visual elements are included only to break up the text. For example, if you're studying Africa and see a picture of a lion, that picture may just be for interest or it may be used to illustrate the wildlife of a particular country.

✓ **Look at the end of the chapter or article for a summary.** Chapters often include a summary section, outlining the key points of the chapter. An article may summarize the main points in the last paragraph.

✓ **For textbook readings, look also for summary or review questions.** Read these to get an idea of what the authors and your instructor think are important ideas. Also use these questions to study for tests. The questions give you some idea of what you should know and be able to answer after completing the reading assignment.

READING FOR THE MAIN IDEAS

After you've previewed the reading, you should have a good idea of the topic, what's covered, how the information is organized, and how the information is related. Now you can read to get a sense of the main ideas of the reading assignment.

You may start by skimming again through the reading assignment and reading the opening paragraph of each main section. You can also read the opening sentence of each paragraph. If you don't do another skim through, focus on key parts of the assignment to find meaning.

Writers usually center each paragraph they write around one central idea. Sometimes, that main idea is expressed in one sentence; you'll hear this called the *topic sentence*. Other times, you need to connect the ideas in two or three different sentences to get the main idea.

Also, the placement of the main idea can vary. It would be convenient if every writer started each new paragraph with the main idea, but that format isn't always the best way to convey information. Often, though, the first sentence does tell you the topic of the paragraph. If not, look elsewhere for the main idea when reading. For example, a text may want to prove a rule, and in doing so may take different approaches. A paragraph might start with examples, and then describe the rule it proves, or the paragraph might start with the rule, and then use the examples to back up the rule.

The introduction, opening paragraph, and opening sentence can usually give you a good idea of the main idea. When you read, keep these ideas in the forefront and relate them to the other information you read. For example, think about each sentence and its role. Is it the main idea? Does it provide an example of the concept? Does it provide supporting information for the main idea? Does it connect the idea or concept to the preceding (or following) information? Does the text provide an *analogy* (where the concept is compared to something similar and familiar to help readers better understand) For example, when working with computers, the hard disk is often compared to a filing cabinet; this is an analogy.

For additional information, look for typical setups for the presentation. For example, common setups include:

✓ Problem followed by solution(s)

✓ Argument followed by supporting reasons

✓ Question(s) followed by answer(s)

✓ Term or concept followed by examples

If it's not clear what the key ideas outlined in the introduction are, ask your instructor for clarification. Of if you think you missed one of the points, ask your instructor to repeat the key concepts.

Try to determine which are the important supporting facts for you to remember. For example, most American students know that Columbus discovered America in 1492; that's considered an important historical fact. The date he left, the actual date he landed, who first spotted land — these details tend not to be as important. Learn to make this distinction about what's important and what's not by listening to what your instructor stresses and through your own experience.

REVIEWING YOUR READING

As you read, frequently review what you've read. Consider the following suggestions.

✓ **Quiz yourself about what you've just read.** What do you remember? What stands out?

Frequent Review

Don't wait until the end of the chapter to review what you've read. Do so more frequently. You have to find the right balance. Paraphrasing every few paragraphs is probably too much. Trying to paraphrase the entire chapter is too little.

All Classes

Don't think only about how the reading relates to that particular subject area. Think also about how it relates to your other classes and other information you know about. For example, history can tell you a lot about the culture of a place (social studies). Math concepts are applied in scientific research and studies. Weather is related to geography.

✓ **Paraphrase what you've read.** *Paraphrasing* is putting something into your own words. See whether you can explain the concept or tell the story using your own words.

✓ **Think about what your instructor is likely to stress in the reading.** What ideas do you think he or she wants you to pay the most attention to?

✓ **Connect what you're reading to what you already know about the subject.** What does this new information add? How is this new information important? Does it introduce something new? Build on something you've already learned? Go into more detail about a general concept?

TAKING NOTES

You may benefit from taking notes on what you're reading. Taking notes — both from a lecture and from a reading — is covered in Chapter 4. When reading, if you have a question, write it down immediately and note the page number or use some other citation so that you can flag the material that provoked your question. You can then look up this question or ask your instructor.

Consider creating an outline of the reading, including the key topics and main ideas. As another method, you may take a more graphical approach and draw a map of the information, showing how the information is related.

If you can mark in your textbook, you may want to highlight. Chapter 10 gives you some guidelines so that you don't highlight too much (or too little). Suffice it to say that the purpose of highlighting is to spot the main concepts at a glance, read the highlighted words or phrases, and get the meaning of the content.

Improving Your Reading Skills

Because reading is such a critical skill, you want to always seek ways to improve your reading. The more you practice, the better. And when you're reading, you can follow a few tips or strategies that will enhance the reading and help you develop your reading skills. These include working on your vocabulary and reading more.

BUILDING YOUR VOCABULARY

The more words you know, the easier and faster you'll be able to read. Your comprehension will also improve. You have a few ways to build your vocabulary. You may take vocabulary as part of your English classes, where you specifically study this topic and seek to learn new terms, understand their meaning, and use them appropriately. If not, you may find that workbooks or flashcards help improve and increase your vocabulary.

To be a good reader, you have to not only be able to quickly recognize words but also know their meaning. Be alert for words that you don't recognize or know the meaning for, and then use a dictionary to look up any words for which you don't know the meaning. Also consider developing your own list of words and their meanings as you go through your readings.

As another option, you may decide to make it a point to learn a set number of new words each day. While you probably wouldn't want to read the dictionary, you can find word-a-day calendars or e-mail messages that can help you learn new words. Or you might make or purchase vocabulary flashcards and make a game of it.

Another tactic when you come across a word you don't know is to guess at the word's meaning based on the sentence. Even if you don't know the word, you can probably figure out its meaning by reviewing how it's used in a sentence. Test your guess against the real meaning by using your dictionary.

"Real" Meaning

Words can have various meanings, as you probably know. Think about a saw you use to cut wood versus saying, "I saw a tree." Words can also have different, subtler meanings or nuances based on how the word is used within a particular sentence; this is known as *connotation* of a word. Be alert to the meanings and connotations of words as you read.

When you paraphrase your reading, learn also to paraphrase terms, especially new terms or words you don't know. Don't just read the dictionary definition, but be able to define the terms using your own words.

Learn to break a word down. Our language is based on previous languages, most commonly Latin and Greek. (Learning the origin of a word is learning its *etymology*.) When you learn different parts of words and how they're combined, you can often guess the meaning of a word. For example, "ology" means "study of" and "theo" means God; therefore, what do you think the word theology would mean?

READ MORE AND BE AN ACTIVE READER

Another way to read better is to read more. If you read a lot, like most things, you get better. So read a variety of different types of writing.

Practice your skimming, too. For example, pick up a newspaper and skim the front page. You can probably immediately retell the main stories of that day. You can apply these same scanning/skimming skills to other reading.

Don't just read, think! Think of questions, anticipate what your instructor may emphasize, and make notes. But also anticipate what's going to happen next. For example, if you're reading about a science experiment, perhaps you can predict the results. If reading literature (covered in the following section), guess the ending. Writing progresses from one idea to the next, so anticipating what will follow helps you make that transition and connect one idea to the next.

In class, when you discuss the reading, be sure to participate. Ask questions. Express your opinion on what you think about the reading. Get clarification for any ideas or concepts that are unclear to you. Listen to what your classmates think about the reading.

Reading Literature

Reading literature (fiction, poetry, memoirs, for example) requires a different approach than reading nonfiction, instructional writing. Meaning in literature isn't often stated directly, but is implied. You have to get a sense on your own of what the work means, instead of having the author explicitly saying, "This is idea 1, and this is idea 2."

Good writers do create stories that are organized and comprehensible. For example, a story usually follows some organization, whether it's told chronologically, in flashbacks, from different perspectives, and so on. Also, writers provide many clues to the meaning or main idea(s) they want you to get from the work. The following sections cover strategies for reading literature.

LOOKING FOR KEY LITERATURE ELEMENTS

When reading literature, you won't be able to skim for meaning. You'll have to look for other important elements to help you. In particular, the following are important to consider when reading literature:

✓ **Characters:** Who are the main characters in the piece? Who is the *narrator*, the person telling the story? Does this person have a bias? That is, can you trust what he or she says? What are the names and roles of the main characters?

✓ **Events and interaction:** What happens in the story? How do the characters interact? How are they related or connected? Why do the characters act or behave the way they do? Why do the events play out as they do?

✓ **Setting:** Where does the piece take place? Is the setting critical to the story? Does the setting provide background? Does the setting give historical, physical, or other information that is key to the story?

✓ **Time:** When does the story take place? Is it timeless (like, for example, some poetry pieces), or is it grounded in a particular place and time (like Crane's story of the Civil War in *The Red Badge of Courage*)?

✓ **Organization:** How is the story organized? Most commonly, stories are told chronologically, but in some works, you may find that the author moves back and forth (in time as well as place).

✓ **Writing style:** What does the writing style tell you about the story? Is the writing richly detailed? Or sparse? (For example, Hemingway was famous for his Spartan writing style.) How does the writing style affect the meaning? Do you have to make assumptions or guesses because there are gaps?

✓ **Symbolism:** Symbolism can be tricky because, sometimes, as the saying goes, "A cigar is just a cigar." Other times, a journey represents something beyond just the trip itself. For example, Tom Sawyer's trip was more about his development as a person than his trip down the river.

✓ **Theme:** What are the themes of the story? What elements or ideas are repeated or emphasized? Think about this throughout your reading, not just at the end. Notice what people, places, and events pop up over and over again.

Experience Grows

As you read more literature, your awareness and ability to spot important symbolism will grow. Also, your instructors should help you spot important details that have meaning beyond their face value.

> ## Don't Understand?
>
> If you don't understand a play or novel, try another medium. For example, rent a movie of a play or novel. Or attend a play in your area. Or use the Internet to find a synopsis of the novel or play.

✓ **Retelling of a story:** Many stories are in some way or form a retelling of a previous story. If you think about Tom Sawyer's trip, you can find other trips from Greek mythology (Homer's *Odyssey*) to the Bible (the trip of the Magi). These are just a few examples.

REVIEWING AND TAKING NOTES ON LITERATURE

Reading literature presents information in a different way than non-fiction reading. An outline, for example, isn't often a good way to take notes about literature. You also can't skim for meaning. What can you do?

One approach that can be helpful is writing a summary. You can summarize the essence of the story or poem, including key characters and details. You can also purchase summaries, like CliffsNotes, of popularly studied literature and topics. While these can be useful study guides, keep in mind that you can't rely on them solely. You still need to do the reading. If you're struggling with a particular work, though, a study guide can help you make sense and get your bearings within the story.

Another way to review literature is to use discussion questions to think more deeply about what you've read. Your instructor may provide questions, or the book itself may include discussion questions. For example, you may be asked to answer a question about a particular event and how it changed the character. You may be asked to think about how the story would have turned out differently if the circumstances were slightly different. You may be asked to keep a literature notebook, in which you record and respond in writing to your discussion questions. And you may decide to do this even when it's not required; it'll help you write papers and study for tests.

Taking Notes

> *What we learn with pleasure we never forget.*

—Alfred Mercier

When you attend a lecture class or an instructor gives you instructions orally, you're expected to take notes. Often, though, no one has taught you how to take notes. You may try to write down everything the instructor says and end up with only bits and pieces of the information. When you realize that you can't possibly record all of the lecture and instruction, you may figure that you can get the material from the book, but often, the instructor covers topics outside the scope of the textbook. So what's next? You may decide to focus only on the most important topics. But what are the most important topics? How do you know where to concentrate your attention when taking notes and what you can leave out?

Taking notes involves active listening, as well as connecting and relating information to ideas you already know. It also involves seeking answers to questions that arise from the material.

While, in the whole scheme of your academic career, taking notes may not seem very important, the truth is that reviewing the content of lectures and readings (that is, reviewing your notes) greatly impacts your grades on tests and papers. Therefore, taking notes has a big impact on your success in school.

This chapter provides you with several note-taking strategies, from listening to clues that help you determine the most important parts of a lecture to revising your notes so that they make sense and become useful study aids for tests. You also see that taking notes isn't just for class lectures but is also useful for recording the key points from reading assignments.

Taking Notes in a Lecture

In many of your classes, your instructor lectures on or makes a presentation about a topic, usually one that's related to the current subject you're studying. Your responsibility as a student in that class is to take notes so that you can remember the key points your instructor makes. The following sections share the wrong (and often most common way) to take notes, and then help you discover the right ways.

THE WRONG WAY TO TAKE NOTES

When taking notes, many students try methods that seem to make sense but in reality don't work well. For example, you may try to write down everything the instructor says, but you'll most likely find that you can't keep up. And even if you could keep up, this method doesn't work well because you're functioning simply as a recorder; you aren't really listening to the information and making connections about the information and the subject at hand.

You may also try tape-recording a lecture, and while this ensures you have a record of everything that is spoken, a recording doesn't take into account any visuals (maps, diagrams, charts, and so on) the instructor may use in the lecture. Also, when you go back to study, you probably won't have time to listen to each and every lecture all over again, which makes the recording less than useful. Finally, when you're recording, you're not actively engaging in thinking about the material. So strike that method.

THE RIGHT WAY TO TAKE NOTES

What's the best way, then, to take notes? The best method is taking notes on paper or in a notebook. This section provides some suggestions using this method for lecture notes. In the "Taking

Notes on Reading Assignments" section later in the chapter, you can find out how useful it is to also take notes on your reading assignments.

Listening for Key Information

When you're listening to a lecture, your goal is to capture the main points, facts, and ideas. One of the first strategies is knowing how to listen for the important information. Your goal is to listen to and think about why the instructor is presenting the information.

✓ Why is it important?

✓ How might that information be used in your class?

✓ How might the information be used on a test?

✓ Is this information a basis for other information?

✓ Could this information be used as content for an essay?

Instead of writing down everything you hear, think about what the information means and why the instructor is lecturing on that subject. Also, don't worry about what your classmates are recording. You may see another student writing furiously and think you should be also. You should learn to trust your own judgment in taking notes and not worry what other students are doing.

When taking notes, also listen and look for clues from your instructor. Instructors often uses several methods to stress the

---

Too Many Notes!

Taking too many notes can be a bad thing. If you've somehow written down all of the information from a lecture, you have simply recorded it, not taken judicious notes on it. You haven't actively listened or made connections. Your focus in taking notes is not to get down every word but to get down the important concepts and facts important information in a lecture. Consider the following verbal and nonverbal clues that usually indicate important information:

✓ **Repeated ideas or themes:** Most instructors repeat key information more than once to stress the importance. They may also preface important information by saying something like, "Now this is important" or "Remember this."

✓ **Information that's written down on the blackboard, overhead transparency, or whiteboard:** When instructors want to stress key points, they often write down key facts or ideas for you to both see and hear. These are usually important.

✓ **Concepts that provide a foundation for other information:** For example, an instructor may introduce key literary terms or concepts that provide the basis for a literary discussion. Or in a science class, an instructor may stress steps or procedures that are followed in experiments. Take note of these concepts and steps.

✓ **Obvious organizational structures:** For example, in the introduction to the lecture, your instructor may say, "I'm going to tell you the four main reasons why the United States entered World War I." You note that there are four main points, and then listen for those four points. Sometimes the instructor reminds you of the points, saying things like, "The second reason why. . . ." Or the instructor may write down the main ideas.

Missing Point?

If you're not clear what the key ideas outlined in the introduction are, ask your instructor for clarification. In the same way, if you think you missed one of the points, ask your instructor to repeat the key concepts outlined at the start of the lecture.

Another way an instructor may present a lecture is in chronological order, citing key dates or events. Again, use this structure to follow along, see how one event led to another, and organize your notes accordingly. And if you find a gap in the timeline, ask your instructor to clarify.

✓ **Tangents:** Sometimes, instructors get off on tangents, with a personal story or experiences. While this may make the information more vivid in your imagination, it's not likely to be something the instructor will include on the test. You usually don't have to record any personal stories or material that's off the subject.

✓ **Instructions that tell you what's expected of you during the course:** For example, your instructor may give you information about the timing and structure of tests, due dates and guidelines for papers, and so on. Usually, an instructor provides a handout for this crucial information, but if not, it's up to you to record these details.

✓ **Handouts:** If the instructor takes the time to create a handout, it usually contains the main ideas, concepts, steps, and so on. If the instructor gives you the handout at the start of the lecture, use it to follow along with the key points. If you receive the handout at the end of class, use it to review what the instructor has stressed.

✓ **Web site content:** Many schools now use course-management systems that provide the students with communication and other tools for the course. For example, your instructor may post the syllabus, handouts, and assignments on the course site. Your instructor may also post a copy of lecture outlines or other information helpful for preparing for class and studying for tests. Pay careful attention to these.

Getting Tips for Taking Notes

Even when you know what's important, it can be difficult to transfer all the important points from a lecture onto a page. You can use the following shortcuts to make note-taking easier.

✓ For lecture notes, include the date, instructor, and title of the lecture (if there is one). You may also include the textbook chapter, part, or pages on which the lecture is based.

✓ If the lecture is based on a reading assignment, make sure you've done the reading and, perhaps, even taken notes on the reading. (Taking notes from reading assignments is covered in the "Taking Notes on Reading Assignments" section later in this chapter.) If you know the material from the reading assignment, you'll have a good idea of the structure of the lecture, as well as the key points.

This helps you decide what to note and what to let pass. Also, if the instructor's lecture is based entirely on the reading assignment, you can refer to the reading assignment as you take notes. And if the instructor adds facts, concepts, or new ideas or if the instructor disagrees with the reading assignment, these are alerts that you should be paying attention and taking notes on these ideas.

✓ If your instructor provides an overview of the lecture, structure your notes in an outline form so that you can understand how the ideas relate. After class, you can (and should) go back and revise your notes if the structure and organization of the lecture isn't clear. (Revising your notes so that they make sense as a whole is covered in the "Organizing Your Notes for Studying" section later in this chapter.)

✓ Instead of trying to record what the instructor says word-for-word, put the ideas into your own words. Paraphrase what the instructor says. At the same time, do note key concepts or terms, even if you don't know what they mean. Flag them to look the meanings up later. If you aren't sure of the spelling, make a note (such as, "sp?") next to the term so that you can go back and check the spelling and/or meaning.

✓ You may not be able to get all the details, but seek to get the main ideas, and then leave blanks to go back and fill in the detail. For example, if the instructor is talking about the five events leading up to the Civil War, it's more important to write down the events than make complete descriptions of each event.

✓ Add your own thoughts about what the information means and how it connects to other concepts you've learned in class. Also record any questions you have (or questions you think the instructor may ask on a test based on the lecture content). For example, in a lecture on Shakespeare, you might discover and note, "I think this theme also occurs in Richard III."

✓ Use abbreviations for common words. You can also use your own abbreviations, as long as you remember what they mean. For example, you might use "pt" to mean point. And you can shorten names to initials. For example, rather than write Napoleon Bonaparte every time, you can write "NB" or just "N."

✓ Leave out time-consuming words like "the," "in," "for," "be," "are," and so on.

Common Abbreviations

Some common abbreviations include the following:

✓ w/ (with)

✓ w/o (without)

✓ b/c (because)

✓ @ (about)

✓ = (equals)

You can also use your own abbreviations as long as you remember what they mean!

✓ You don't have to use complete sentences. For example, you may jot down "Halle Berry = first actress of color to win Best Actress Oscar."

✓ Use a graphical structure for your notes (for example, indenting lines, drawing arrows, using bullets) to show how information is related.

Taking Notes on Reading Assignments

In many classes, the lecture is based on content from a book. For example, in a literature class, you need to read the novel or play or poem first so that you can follow along with the lecture. In a history class, you need to read the chapters about the end of the Cold War so that you can better understand and follow the lecture on this topic.

Instructors don't always cover only the information from the book. Often, they add other facts because an instructor who simply lectures from the book makes for a pretty boring lecturer. The best lecturers bring in other concepts and show how concepts relate to other events or trends or ideas. They help you build connection and see relationships among the topic at hand and the world at large. That's why it's important that you take notes on lectures (as covered in the preceding sections).

In addition to lecture notes, you should also take notes on any reading assignments. Doing so will help you find and note the key ideas in the reading materials. Taking notes on a reading assignment ensures that you are really understanding the information rather than just skimming over it. Having these notes will come in handy when you need to prepare for a test or compose a paper. The following sections give you tips on how to best take notes on your class reading assignments.

To Highlight or Not to Highlight?

You'll find differing opinions on the usefulness of highlighting. It's true that if you indiscriminately highlight entire passages (maybe even the whole book), the highlighting won't help much when you go back to review the main concepts. Also some anti-highlighters say that highlighting makes for passive rather than active reading. This is similar to jotting down everything the instructor says but without making sense of it yourself.

Personally, I like to highlight (as do a lot of instructors and students), but when highlighting, it does make sense to do so judiciously. Consider these guidelines for highlighting:

✓ **Focus on the main point — and that may not be the entire sentence.** It's perfectly okay to highlight only key terms or parts of sentences. In fact, you may get a better sense of the main idea of a paragraph if you highlight a string of words (excluding extraneous information) that lets you glean the main idea at a glance.

✓ **Consider reading the entire paragraph, and then going back and highlighting the important words and ideas.** If you highlight from the start, you may not be sure of the paragraph's purpose and how to best capture that purpose or idea with your highlighter.

✓ **Don't make highlighting more complex than it needs to be.** Some students use several color of highlighters to call attention to different types of information. This is overkill and is likely to add confusion (rather than clarity) when you do review this information. Also, this makes taking notes more time-consuming.

✓ **If you buy a used textbook or other reading material, look for one with little or no highlighting.** It's hard to ignore the previous owner's highlighting.

Note the Page Number

When making notes based on a reading assignment, note the chapter and page number. This enables you to go back to that section and review, especially if it ends up being a section you had questions about.

✓ **In addition to highlighting, consider jotting notes in the margins, next to passages.** This note-taking strategy is covered in detail in the following section.

MAKING NOTES IN YOUR TEXTBOOK

You may have grown up with admonition to never write in a textbook or novel, but that changes as you progress through higher levels of school. And yes, marking in a textbook can affect its resale value, but it can also help you review information and note your thoughts as you read the material. If you're adamant about keeping your textbook free from markings, consider keeping a reader's notebook, in which you can cite the page and passage, and then record your thoughts in this notebook.

The purpose of notes isn't so much to remind you of what the passage or paragraph says but to record your ideas and questions. What do you make of this point? Does it relate to something you learned earlier in class (or in another class)? Look for ways to connect what you're reading to what you've read in other places in that textbook or in other course books or classes.

Also consider jotting down questions you have, especially if you don't understand a word or a concept. You can then either ask the instructor for clarification or research the idea on your own.

Most instructors welcome questions; it shows that students are engaged in the learning process. So in both lecture and reading notes, you may want to record any questions you have for the instructor:

✓ You may need more information to better understand the reasoning behind a concept.

✓ You may wonder how one event related to another event.

✓ You may, at times, even ask whether certain information is important. (Some instructors tell you that certain material will not be on the test, for whatever reason.)

> ## On the Test?
>
> Don't get in the habit of badgering the instructor about each and every point you cover in class and whether it will be on a test or used in an assignment. You can, however, ask this question when the information is really detailed, seems like an aside (or extra information) from the main point, or isn't covered in class. Instructors usually consider these questions to be legitimate clarification of what's important on the test and what's not.

RECORDING READING NOTES IN A NOTEBOOK

If you don't want to mark up your textbook with questions or you don't have room enough in the book to jot down your thoughts and ideas, consider keeping a reader's notebook to record your notes, questions, and comments. As the following section discusses, it's a good idea to rework your notes from both the lecture and reading into an easy-to-scan format. Doing so organizes the information and stresses the important facts so that you can use this information for studying for tests, finishing homework assignments, or writing papers.

Even if you write notes in the book itself, you may also use a reading notebook. You'll have more room to record your thoughts and any questions you have. You'll also have space to draw connections from one section to another.

Like jotting notes, comments, and questions, you may also jot down the main ideas, especially to help organize the information. The headings and subheadings in a chapter can help you see how the information is related and its relative importance to other concepts in the chapter, and you can note this in your notebook. You might include the headings in the notes, or organize the notes in an outline format that follows the chapter organization. You can also flag any charts, diagrams, pictures, illustrations, or other artwork that concisely summarizes material and shows its relevance to other material. You can note the page number of the illustration or flag the page with a Post-it note.

Taking Notes Before Class

In addition to using a notebook, consider one more suggestion for effective note-taking: do your reading assignments and take your notes before class. If you do so, you'll have a much easier time following the lecture, because you have a good idea of not only how the information is structured but also what content will be covered in class. You can also see what the instructor stresses (and omits or adds).

Organizing Your Notes for Studying

You take notes from lectures and readings for a purpose: to study from them or to use them to complete an assignment (such as a paper, for example). While you may think at first that reading and attending class is just busywork — a waste of your time — if you put the effort into good note-taking, you'll see how much easier it is to study for upcoming tests or other assignments. There's one last step for note-taking and that includes reviewing and, if needed, reorganizing your notes so that they are easy to use for studying.

When you're preparing for a test, you have many resources to study from: lecture notes, textbook readings, and any notes from your reading. Often, these overlap. Or one element (like lecture notes) provides an overview, while another element (the textbook) provides the necessary details.

Rather than studying from all these various sources, consider getting into the habit of reviewing and reorganizing your notes into one comprehensive, organized, concise, and complete set of notes. The end result not only helps you better prepare for the test, but the actual act of compiling, arranging, and reviewing the notes also acts as an effective method to help you see connections and create a complete picture from disparate parts.

COMPILING YOUR NOTES

You can use any number of methods to create a review sheet. Consider some of the following:

✓ Type up your notes from the various sources, putting "like" information together. Ideally, you want to review your notes soon after the class and fill in any gaps.

✓ Create an outline of the key points, and then fill in the details under the main and subpoints.

✓ Use a two-column grid. On the left hand, write questions you have (or questions you think may be asked). On the right hand side, briefly list the answers to the questions.

If you use a column method to list questions, but don't know the answer, flag areas where you need to do more research in the left column. You can then find the answers either in your textbook, from your instructor or in a study group.

✓ Use visual mapping methods to record the main idea and then show how other themes, concepts, and facts relate and tie together with this subject area. A visual map is like a graphic outline; you write the information in a way that illustrates how the ideas relate.

For instance, you usually start with a main idea written in the center of the paper. You then add key facts to the main idea, using lines to connect them. For the key facts, you can add other supporting information underneath or connected with lines.

ANTICIPATE QUESTIONS

When you read through your notes and own thoughts, think about how the instructor may test you on your knowledge of this topic. If you were the instructor, what questions would you ask that would demonstrate that your students have a good understanding of the key facts? Often, good students already have an idea of what test questions may be and prepare accordingly. But this is a skill that you can learn and improve by trying yourself to guess appropriate test questions.

Once you think of the question, see whether your notes provide the answer. If not, look back through your notes and reading assignments to find the answer and then include that material in your study notes. For some detailed questions, for instance, essay questions, you may want to create an outline of the response. In doing so, you may need to pull information from different sections of your notes to create a cohesive answer. When you study, you can practice answering questions using your notes.

Sharing and Comparing Notes with Classmates

One helpful way to study for tests or review content is to create and work with a study group. If you're in a study group, compare notes among your group to see whether you missed anything. You can even take turns condensing and organizing the notes from a lecture into a study sheet for the group. You learn more about study groups in Chapter 5.

If you miss a class, get lecture notes from a classmate. Ask someone in class that you know takes good notes or e-mail other students in the class to ask for a copy of notes. You may in fact want to get a few sets of notes instead of relying on just one other student. Also, check your course Web site (if you have one) for lecture outlines or forum discussions about a topic.

Recognizing the Benefits of Taking Note

You know the hows and whys of note-taking. To end this chapter, read the following list of reasons why taking notes is so important.

✓ Taking notes helps you better understand the concepts and reinforces your learning and understanding. This, in turn, improves your ability to remember the important aspects of the topic.

✓ Effectively taking notes (instead of just writing down every word) helps you look for meaning, patterns, connections, and relations among concepts in this class as well as in other classes.

These are skills that are critical as you progress through school. For example, in college, it's expected that students have some idea of how to find meaning, look for patterns, and connect information not only within a particular course but also to other courses.

✓ Taking notes in class can help you concentrate instead of daydreaming!

✓ Good notes improve your chances of getting good grades on tests and assignments.

Studying for Tests

" We are not what we know but what we are willing to learn. "

—Mary Catherine Bateson

No one really enjoys tests, but they are part and parcel of school. What is your attitude toward taking a test? Are you committed to doing your best? Are you overwhelmed? Do you study only at the last minute?

Attitude and preparation are key to successfully passing tests, and like the other skills in this book, you can learn to improve your test-taking skills. This chapter focuses on how to make the most of your study time; Chapter 6 covers some strategies for particular kinds of tests (such as literature or math) and test questions.

Several of the preceding chapters in this book lead up to taking tests. In Chapter 3, you discover how to do and take notes on reading assignments. In Chapter 4, you read about techniques for taking effective notes. These are both skills that you need to prepare for the test. Other than that, this chapter covers other basic preparation. In this chapter, you find that when you feel prepared to take a test, successfully passing the test becomes infinitely more manageable and less stressful.

Anticipating the Test and Its Questions

The first thing to do to prepare for a test is to gather as much information as possible about the test itself. Doing so helps you know what you need to study, how much time you have to prepare, what types of questions you can anticipate, and more. This section focuses on finding out the details of a test and applying this information when you begin your review (covered in the "Reviewing for a Test" section later in this chapter).

Most of the time, your instructor will give you advance warning for major tests and may even provide some guidelines of what to expect. If not, ask your instructor any questions you have about the test. Also, after you take one test from an instructor, you'll know what to expect on the future tests — for example, whether she uses questions based on the book and/or focuses on homework assignments.

Your instructor may even give you a study guide or host a study session in class. These are helpful guides when studying for a test, so pay close attention to what the instructor stresses in these guides or sessions.

The following sections look at specific questions you want to ask about your tests.

WHAT TYPE OF TEST?

Instructors use different kinds of tests, and some tests are better than others for seeing what you know and don't know. For example, in math tests, you'll typically solve problems, so it'd be unusual to have an essay question on a math test. On the other hand, in literature, expect to find essay questions, multiple choice, matching, fill-in-the-blank, and so on.

Ask your instructor what kind of test you'll have. Is it an essay exam? Does it contain multiple-choice items? A matching list? A combination of elements? Your instructor should give you some idea of the types of questions you can expect. The following lists the most common types of assessment or test items.

✓ **True/false:** Probably one of the most basic test items, this type of question makes a statement. As the test-taker, you evaluate that statement and say whether it is true or false. For example, on a history or social studies test, your instructor may ask "True or false: Benedict Arnold was a successful merchant trader." (The answer is true.) Sometimes, these questions take a slightly different format, such as yes/no or on/off.

✓ **Multiple choice:** In this type of question, the instructor writes a statement, and then provides several possible answers. You select the best answer from the list. For example, your instructor may ask this question:

Who wrote "To Kill a Mockingbird?"

a. Victor Hugo

b. Harper Lee

c. Mark Twain

d. Tennessee Williams

(The answer is b.) Sometimes, several of the answers are correct (or none is). For example, answer "d" could have read "all of the above" or "none of the above." Chapter 6 explains how to evaluate and be alert for these possibly tricky questions.

✓ **Fill-in-the-blank:** For other questions, the instructor may just provide the statement, but not any possible answers. For example, the preceding question might appear as "_____ wrote *To Kill a Mockingbird*" or "Who wrote *To Kill a Mockingbird?*" You fill in the blank part to complete the statement or answer the questions. (In this case, Harper Lee.)

✓ **Matching questions:** Another type of question you find on exams requires you to match items from one list to items in a second list. For example, on a vocabulary test, the instructor may list the terms in one list and the definitions in the

Short Essay

Your instructor may distinguish between *short* and regular essay questions. For example, in a short essay question, you may write only a paragraph to answer the question. For a more detailed essay question, you may need to write several paragraphs. The test should give you guidelines on the appropriate length for your response.

second. You then match them up. Usually, one list is numbered and one is lettered, so you write the matching letter next to the number. As a younger child, you may remember drawing an arrow from one item to its match, another way to supply the answer.

✓ **Essay questions:** For topics that require an expression of your thoughts and ideas (for example, talking about the theme in a novel), your instructor may ask you to write an essay question. For example, a question may say, "Talk about the importance of setting (time and place) in *To Kill a Mockingbird*." You then compose your response.

Students often struggle with essay questions, but if you know how to prepare for them (as explained in Chapter 6), you'll be confident in answering this type of test item.

✓ **Problems:** On math tests, you often have to solve a problem and provide the correct answer. For example, in algebra, you might need to solve an equation. In geometry, you may need to write a proof for a statement. You may be graded solely on the getting the right answer, or you be graded on a combination of showing your work and providing the right answer (often called *partial credit*, because you can get some credit for the work you do without getting the right answer).

✓ **Performances:** For some classes, your grade may be based on performance. For example, in biology, you may have to dissect a frog and identify its parts. In a music class, you may have to play a song on an instrument. In a physical education class, you may have to perform a dance or play a sport as part of your grade. While these may not seem like "tests," they are assessment methods that instructors use in particular situations. You find out more about preparing for performance-based assessments in Chapter 6.

WHAT'S COVERED ON THE TEST?

In addition to figuring out what type of test you can expect, find out what's covered on the test. Is the test on just one unit? Or is it *cumulative* (that is, it covers all the preceding units). Does the test cover just the reading from the textbook? Or should you also review outside reading resources and/or lecture notes?

Usually, your instructor tells you that a particular test covers certain chapters or a page range in your textbook or other reading material. Don't focus only on the textbook, though. Know what other resources the instructor may use for questions. Gather all these resources when you're preparing to study, so that what you need is at your fingertips.

Study Breaks

One of the advantages of studying early is that you won't feel the time pressure to get the studying done in one session. Break your study time into two or more sessions or take frequent breaks. There's only a certain amount of information you'll be able to absorb in one sitting, so try to plan enough time that you can at least take breaks to refresh your mind when studying.

WHEN IS THE TEST (OR HOW LONG DO YOU HAVE TO STUDY)?

Another factor to take into consideration is when the test is scheduled; that is, how much time do you have to study? Sometimes, an instructor provides you with a schedule or syllabus of all the test dates; this may be for a quarter, semester, or the entire school year. Other times, the instructor may announce tests as you progress through the materials.

In any case, you can make the most of your preparation time by doing the following:

✓ **Complete your reading assignments.** One of the biggest mistakes is to put off doing your reading until the last minute. When you do that, you have to not only study but also read, and most people don't have time for both. It's key that you do your reading (and homework) when it's due. You'll be able to more actively participate in class and, therefore, the information should be easier for you to recall, come test time.

✓ **Take good notes.** Chapter 4 is devoted to note-taking; as covered in that chapter, consider taking notes not only on lectures but also on reading assignments.

✓ **Do your homework assignments.** Often, you practice skills on a test in homework drills, especially in classes like math. If you don't do your homework or don't put a lot of effort into it, you're likely to struggle at test time. Practice helps you improve; do your homework!

HOW WILL THE TEST BE GRADED?

Knowing what criteria the instructor will use to grade the test is another question to ask when preparing for the test. For example, math instructors may give partial credit if you show your work, even if you aren't accurate in your final answer to a problem. Your instructor may tell you ahead of time or indicate on the test itself the relevant weight or number of points given for a right response

Grading on the Curve

You may have heard the expression "grading on a curve," and some instructors may use this type of grading (called officially norm-referenced grading) especially when everyone does poorly on a test. Because educational studies have emphasized the drawbacks of this type of grading, instructors are discouraged from using this style of grading. Grading on a curve, because of its comparative nature, encourages competition and doesn't encourage cooperation.

in each test section (if there is more than one type of question). For example, true and false questions may be worth one point, while a more difficult question, like an essay question, may be worth 15 points. Often, the instructor uses a grading scale of 100% (perfect score), but you may find instructors who use a different method for grading.

Also, note whether the instructor will subtract if you guess. Are you penalized for wrong answers? Is it okay to take a guess? The key is to know what the instructor expects from you and what you need to provide to get the best grade.

In addition to knowing how the test will be scored, you also want to know how the test will affect your grade in that class. For example, if there are four tests given in a marking period and the instructor includes homework and participation, the instructor may break your grade down as follows:

Test 1	20% of grade
Test 2	20% of grade
Test 3	20% of grade
Test 4	20% of grade
Homework	10% of grade
Class work	10% of grade

From this scoring method, you can see the importance of each test; each one is worth one-fifth of your grade.

Reviewing for a Test

Why go to all the bother of learning about the test itself? Because doing so helps you know how to review and prepare for the test. You want to make the most effective use of your time and focus on the most important information. And you can best do this by gathering as much information as possible for the test. Armed with a good idea of what you can expect, you can start to review.

This section focuses on how to best review the information that will be covered on a particular test.

REVIEWING READINGS

If your test will cover readings (for example, from a textbook or novel), you want first to complete the readings when they're assigned. Second, take notes on the reading (covered in Chapter 4). Then you should be prepared to study.

When reviewing what you've read, consider the following suggestions:

✓ **Read through your reading notes and quiz yourself.** What do you remember without too much effort? What facts or elements stand out?

✓ **Ask yourself the six main journalism questions and see whether you can answer them about the topic.** The questions include: what? who? when? where? why? how?

✓ **Look at the review questions (if any) in the book to get an idea of what the textbook author thought was important.** See whether you can easily answer these. Flag any questions you don't know.

✓ **If you're able to highlight in your book, read through the highlighted parts to get the main ideas.** Think about how you may be tested on these ideas.

✓ **Imagine that you're the instructor.** What questions would you ask? What facts would you stress?

✓ **Rather than review material and try to memorize it, take a more active approach.** Experience the concept; imagine an idea's consequences; apply the learning. The "Final Tips on Studying for Your Test" section in this chapter covers tips on studying more actively (versus passively trying to memorize and recite back what you've read).

✓ **Think about what you don't know about the subject.** Are there any gaps in your information? Do you have any questions? If you start studying early and notice a gap, you have time to ask the instructor for clarification in class. If, on the other hand, you start studying the night before a test, you may want to look up the information yourself — in your textbook, in another resource, online, and so on. Take special care to do this if you've missed class(es) or feel there are key points you don't understand.

Experience Grows

The first test is somewhat of a dive into the unknown, but after that (if your instructor is consistent), you'll have a good idea of what information the instructor stresses from the materials or lectures, which types of questions the instructor likes to ask, and what other test or assessment elements may appear. Use each test experience to guess or anticipate what the following tests will be like.

Missing Notes

If you missed a class and your instructor gave key lectures at that time, borrow and copy a classmate's notes. This is especially important if you missed any review or study guide sessions in which the instructor specifically reviewed information that will be on the upcoming test.

REVIEWING LECTURE NOTES

In addition to your reading notes, also review your lecture notes (if the lectures are covered on the test). Chapter 4 covers how to listen for and note the main ideas in a lecture. Good notes equal good test preparation.

Read through your lecture notes and, like reviewing your reading notes, anticipate the types of ideas and concepts that are likely to be covered on the test. Try to remember what the instructor stressed. What did she write on the board? What did he talk about more than once?

PRACTICING

For some types of test, you won't be memorizing and reviewing information you've read, but will instead be solving problems (math) or giving a recital (music). In this case, the best way to prepare is to practice. Practicing is also a good way to study for essay answers.

For math, for example, practice solving problems, especially those you got wrong on homework assignments. You're likely to find extra problems (similar to those you did on homework or in class) in your textbook or workbook. The *Cliffs Study Solver* series (Wiley) presents subject-area content review plus loads of practice questions and answers on a wide variety of subject areas. Your instructor may also give you worksheets. Some math courses provide practice problems on a special disc or Internet download. You can work out the solutions, and then check your work using the software and files provided on the coursework. The available materials vary, depending on your school, the course, and other factors, such as whether you have access to computers.

Final Tips on Studying for Your Test

So you've prepared and practiced. What else should you know before you dive in and take your test? Consider these final tips on how to most effectively study for a test:

✓ **Focus on your weak areas.** Look through homework or notes and find the areas you don't understand or the problems that you struggled with. Rather than waste time studying what you already know, focus on what you don't know and need to know.

✓ **Set up a study group of students of similar abilities and similar motives.** Studying in groups is more fun than studying alone; you can create games and quiz each other. Also, in a group, you get different perspectives on the information. If you create a study group, you can select a time, meeting place, and interval for the group to meet. When considering who you want to join the group, make sure you all have the same achievement goals. For example, if everyone in the group is striving for an "A," you don't want a student in your group who'd be thrilled with a "C."

✓ **Share information even if you don't study in a group.** Remember there aren't a limited number of "A's" available. Strive for a cooperative attitude with your classmates. Help them out when you can, and they'll do the same in return. For example, if you're not a good note-taker, you may ask to borrow and copy from someone who does take notes so that you can see what good notes look like.

✓ **Rather than memorize facts, use a better method for recalling information.** For example, you might create a song, tell a story, conceptualize the idea as a picture, create a rhyme, or use a mnemonic device (usually a sentence in which the first letter reminds you of a particular word or phrase).

To create a *mnemonic device*, take the first letter of every word, and then create a sentence to help you recall those words. This method is great when there's information you do need to memorize. For example, to remember the order of the planets (Mercury, Venus, Earth, Mars, Jupiter, Saturn, Uranus, Neptune, and Pluto), you might create a sentence like "My very educated mother just served us nine pizzas."

✓ **Experience the idea in as much detail as possible.** Engage all your senses and imagine what you see, hear, taste, feel, or touch.

✓ **Quiz yourself throughout your assignments, not just before tests.** Doing so not only helps you study but at the same time improves your memory and recall skills.

✓ **Relate the information to other ideas or subjects.** For example, how are two topics similar? Different? How do two topics depend on each other? Does one cause the other? For example, think about how a country's history (for instance, the French Revolution) affects its culture or literature.

✓ **Apply the information.** The information you most easily recall is information that's relevant and useful in everyday situations in life. For example, learning the multiplication tables is pure memorization, but you can probably do multiplication in your head to figure out how much an item is at a 50-percent-off sale, how much tip to leave, and so on. A good instructor strives to teach and stress relevant and applicable skills. If not, look on your own for ways to apply your knowledge. Here's another example: Think about what you know about germs or vitamins when you brush your teeth.

✓ **Learn to apply conceptual information (ideas) as well as procedural (steps or processes).** Math is usually a *procedural application;* history is *conceptual.* For example, you might apply information or ideas to current events, movies, TV programs, news features, and so on. Think about Darwin's theory of evolution and the "survival of the fittest." How is this theory played out (or not played out) in popular TV contests such as *Survivor* or *The Apprentice?* As another example, you may have seen the popular movie *The Matrix.* Does it remind you of any other stories you know, from the Bible, perhaps?

✓ **Don't waste time worrying.** When you're prepared, you'll feel confident, and this positive attitude will come in handy when you tackle the test.

Taking Tests

> *Whether you tell yourself you can or you can't, you are right.*
>
> —Henry Ford

You don't have to hate or dread tests; instead, you can change how you prepare for and approach tests, and as a result, improve your performance. In addition, after you've done well on a few tests, you'll find that test-taking gets easier and easier (although you still have to do the work and study). That's why it's well worth the time to look into ways to improve both your mental preparation and test-taking skills, which are covered in this chapter.

Previous chapters have covered some key skills you need for taking tests, including doing reading assignments (Chapter 3), taking notes (Chapter 4), and preparing for tests (Chapter 5). This chapter focuses on taking the test itself. How can you best spend your time? How can you make sure you get the best grade? What routine should you use when starting a test? This chapter answers these questions and more about the actual taking of a test.

Final Preparation

Chapter 5 covers how to prepare and study for a test. This section focuses on some last-minute ways to prepare, including getting yourself ready physically (eating a good breakfast, for example) and mentally (reviewing your notes). Review the tips in the following sections to find out what you need to do right before your test.

Preparing Mentally and Physically

Your attitude toward test-taking has an effect on your performance. If you let yourself get upset or worry too much, you just end up wasting time. Instead, spend the time preparing. Also, if you tell yourself over and over, "I'm going to do horribly on this test" or "I'm awful at tests," you're likely to fulfill your own prophesy. Instead, think positively and prepare wisely. Doing so will enable you to relax.

Also make sure you get a good night's sleep the night before the test. That means no late-night cramming! Instead, use your study time wisely so that you just need to do a final review (covered in the following section) the night of the test. Don't put off your reading assignments, either; complete all your homework and reading assignments when they are assigned. Doing so makes sure you don't have any leftover work to finish when preparing for a test.

Remember, too, that your brain needs nutrition. Eat a good breakfast, and if the test is in the afternoon, eat a good lunch, too. Drink plenty of fluids — juice or water. Try to avoid caffeine, especially if you tend to get nervous during test time.

Finally, breathe!

Studying the Material

Start studying well in advance of the test so that last night before the test, you can focus on reviewing just a few key areas. After this study session, you can do a last-minute review as your final preparation. In particular, consider the following focused study session (if you've done the detailed review discussed in Chapter 5) as your last and final review:

✓ **Skim through your notes, both from lectures and readings.** You may want to prepare a little mini-sheet that condenses all of the key information onto one study page; this is often recommended, but can take time. Do this only if you're good

Too Early

It's possible to study too early and forget the information, especially if you don't do a final review. When possible, have an intense study session within a few days of the exam; do a final review the night before the test.

at choosing the most important factors and are confident that your condensed guide will summarize enough of what you need to know.

✓ **If your instructor provided a study guide, use that as the basis for your final quick review.** This guide will include the facts and concepts that the instructor thinks are important and should provide a good basis for your studying.

✓ **If the test includes problems to solve (math or science, for example), do a few practice problems.** Think of this as a warm-up, similar to shooting some practice shots or practicing your rebounds before a basketball game.

✓ **If the test will be an essay test, think about what questions the instructor is likely to ask.** Review what you think are the main ideas. If your book includes essay or discussion questions, use them to practice. You don't need to write the entire answer, but consider jotting down a quick outline of the answer. (See the "Essay Questions" section later in this chapter for specific skills for handling essay questions.)

AVOIDING TEST "JITTERS"

Some people get particularly nervous before a test; some even break into hives or have panic attacks. If you think you have a case of test jitters, use the following strategies for coping:

✓ **Remember that having the jitters isn't a life sentence.** Just because you've had the jitters before doesn't mean you have to get them for every test. You can learn to relax and avoid the jitters. Part of that process is believing that you can overcome any fear you have of test-taking by preparing yourself mentally and physically.

✓ **Make sure you get plenty of rest.** Your body is more likely to react adversely if you're tired, ate too much junk food, drank too much caffeine, or have neglected your body in other ways. Cigarettes, alcohol, and drugs are especially damaging not only to test scores, but also — and far more importantly — to your health and future.

✓ **Prepare as well as you can.** When you're prepared, you're less likely to panic. Feeling confident in the material helps you relax.

✓ **Focus on success.** The more success you have on your tests, the more confidence you'll have. This success will grow as you experience less stress and more success, and you can build on these positive experiences to change how you deal with tests.

✓ **If you have extreme reactions, seek the help of a counselor** (either at your school or outside of school) to help you deal with the stress of taking tests. Your counselor may, for example, teach you relaxation techniques to use when you feel test anxiety. Or your counselor may provide other insight, feedback, and other suggestions on dealing with your anxiety.

✓ **Talk to your instructors,** especially if your stress level is having a big impact on how well you do. For example, if you know the material but tend to freeze up, consider talking to the instructor. (If you don't know the material and freeze up, wait until you're prepared and experience a case of jitters. Your "jitters" could just be from a lack of preparation.) Your instructor is more likely to be sympathetic if he or she knows that you've prepared and know the material, but then panicked during the test. Your instructor may provide some alternatives for taking the tests after he or she is aware of your situation.

Missed a Test?

If you miss a test, make arrangements with your instructor to take a make-up test as soon as possible. You might e-mail or leave a message the day you're out (or, even better, the day before), especially if you want to find out whether you will be expected to take the test the day you return. Keep in mind that most instructors do expect you to make up the test the day you come back to class.

Taking the Actual Test

When you're handed the actual test, don't just start blasting away. Doing so usually creates more anxiety because you haven't planned your attack. Instead, approach the test with a plan, as detailed in the following sections.

SKIMMING THE TEST

When you receive the test from your instructor, follow these three steps to quickly preview the test, see what it contains, and budget your time:

1. **Skim through the test and note the types of questions and the length of the test.** Doing so helps you determine the best place to start and how much time you need for each section.

2. **Read the directions and/or listen carefully to the instructor's oral instructions.** Then follow the instructor's instructions exactly. There's no use losing points just because you didn't read the directions or follow instructions. For example, if you are supposed to show your work on a math test and do not, your instructor may penalize you.

3. **Ask any questions about the test itself.** Another reason for skimming through the test is to see whether you have any questions. The time to ask these questions is *before* the test, if possible. If you are unsure how much time you have to complete the test, ask.

DECIDING WHERE TO START
AND WHAT TO ANSWER

After you've reviewed the test, you can decide where to start. It's usually best to start at the beginning and move through the test sequentially, but if the test starts off with a difficult question that you're unsure of, start with an easier problem or section. Skimming through the test before you begin allows you to decide where to start.

When you start answering questions, focus on answering the questions you do know. For those you don't know, you may guess and indicate with some notation (such as a question mark) the ones you think you know, or you might leave blank the questions about which you have no idea. Answering questions you know and moving on not only builds confidence but also gets your mind thinking about the topic and making connections. You may find that you remember other facts and statements as you read through and answer the questions you're sure of. When you go back to check the guesses and answer any questions you skipped, you may have a better idea of the answers.

If the test includes an essay question, be sure to budget enough time to complete that part. Often, the essay question (or hardest question, even if it isn't an essay) is last. You don't want to get to the end of the test and have only five minutes to complete a major part of the test. Again, skimming beforehand gives you some idea of what's in the different test sections so that you can budget your time.

If the test includes problems, take your time solving each one. Show your work, even if you do so on scrap paper. When you check the problems, you want to be able to clearly see each part you solved, so write legibly.

Budget time to review and check your answers. You don't want silly mistakes to affect your grade, so go over all your answers at least one final time.

CHECKING YOUR TEST

After you've completed the test, go through and review your work. Check all your answers, and correct any incorrect answers. Also complete any blank answers (unless you meant to leave them blank). Most instructors don't penalize for guessing, and if that's the case, complete all questions even if you do guess. But check with your instructor if you think incorrect guesses will subtract from your score.

If the test includes problems to solve, check your work carefully. It's easy to *transpose* (flip) a number or make some other easy mathematical mistake. That's why you should write your work out legibly on scrap paper (or on the test if you're supposed to show your work), so that you can double-check each step or calculation.

If the test includes any essay questions, read through your written work and correct any spelling or grammatical mistakes. Make sure your writing is legible, too. You can cross out and neatly write in any changes you need to make.

Clearly Wrong

If you're second-guessing an answer and are unsure whether your first response or second thought is right, stick with your first response. Your first response is usually based on some type of reasoning and is often correct. On the other hand, if the answer is clearly wrong or you're more sure of another response upon reviewing the problem, make the change.

Evaluating Your Test Score

The test process doesn't end with your turning in the test to the instructor. Instead, the last step is to evaluate how you did on the test when the instructor returns the graded test to you. Look at the questions you missed. Did you not know the information? Did you make an easy mistake? Was it a trick question? Read any comments the instructor made. For example, did the instructor make any editing marks on your essay that can help you improve your writing?

Reviewing the test after it has been graded is useful for many reasons. First, you can see what you did well on (and what you didn't know). Second, you can see what types of questions the instructor likes to include as well as what types of questions you struggle with. Third, you can see what topics and subjects the instructor stressed in the test. You can use this knowledge when you prepare for your next test.

Strategies for Typical Test Questions

To help you improve your grades, you should consider some tips on how to tackle typical test questions. You can approach questions (such as true-or-false or multiple choice) with specific strategies for evaluating the question and finding the right answer. This section shares some special techniques for answering common types of test items.

TRUE-OR-FALSE QUESTIONS

When faced with true-or-false questions, keep the following tip in mind:

✓ **Read the statement carefully.** Often, one word can change a statement to true or false, so make sure you don't skip over that word.

✓ **Be on the lookout for key words that often signify a statement is false.** Common qualifier words include "always," "never," "all," "only," "every," and "none." It's usually difficult for "all" of something to be true — for example, "All Southerners are Democrats" — or something to be the "only" cause or reason — for example, taxation was the only cause of the American Revolution.

✓ **If you have to guess, guess true.** True statements are easier to compose, so statistically, tests usually include more true statements.

✓ **Don't look for a pattern; there's unlikely to be one.** Also, don't try to read more into the question. Your instructor isn't likely to ask trick questions (at least you hope not!).

MULTIPLE CHOICE QUESTIONS

With multiple choice questions, you get to see possible answers; it's just a matter of picking the right one from the list. When answering these types of questions, consider the following suggestions:

✓ **Anticipate the answer, and then look for it (or a close match) in the list of possible answers.** Doing so will help you spot the correct answer and give you the confidence that you chose correctly (without second guessing yourself).

✓ **If you don't know the answer, read all the responses.** If one stands out as correct, select that one. If you aren't sure, try to eliminate the ones that are incorrect. Often, you can find the right answer by eliminating those that are wrong. Or at least you can improve your odds if you have to make a guess.

✓ **Look for qualifier words and eliminate any incorrect answers.** See the preceding section for a list of words to watch for. Also, look for answers that don't make sense or that talk about a totally different subject. You can usually eliminate these answers.

The Answer Is a Number

If the answer is a number, experts have found that the highest and lowest numbers are not usually the right answers. If you have to guess, choose one of the middle numbers.

✓ **If more than one answer is correct (or none seems correct),** check for a choice that says "all of the above" or "none of the above." Also, if you see this as one of the possible answers, be sure to double-check your response to make sure it's not "all" or "none." For "all," keep in mind that if you're sure even one of the answers is incorrect, you know that the answer isn't "all."

✓ **The hardest questions are those when the answer isn't** exactly correct, but you're instructed to choose the "best" answer. The trick is to choose the one that you think your instructor would say was the best answer.

MATCHING QUESTIONS

For matching questions, you have two lists and must match each item in one list to an item in the second list (such as definitions or descriptions of events or people). A few tips will help you master matching questions:

✓ **Count the items to see whether the lists are equal.** Most often, all items are used in both lists, and each item is used just once. This can help you match up answers you don't know. If there are an unequal amount of questions and answers, realize that the answer list includes some responses that don't have a match.

✓ **Match those you know first.** When you make a match, cross the answer off the list of possible matches (if your test is structured such that items are used only once). Then proceed to those you think you know. When you're left with those you don't know, you can then guess from the final selections. You've narrowed the choices, so making a guess should be easier.

✓ **If you go through the list and end up with one match that just can't possibly be true, note that at least one of the matches you've made is incorrect.** Try to find the closest match to one of the items (the question or answer) of the one you're sure is wrong, and then make any adjustments.

✓ **Cover up other answers.** If you have a hard time concentrating because of all the available choices, focus on one item from one question or answer list. You can even cover the other items with a piece of paper. Then review the list of possible matches. Doing so can keep you from becoming confused with all the possibilities on both lists.

FILL-IN-THE-BLANK QUESTIONS

Fill-in-the-blank questions are an all-or-nothing kind of question, because you don't have any possible answers to choose from, and you don't have the added advantage of including the information you do know (as you do with an essay question, covered in the

Arranging or Organizing Questions

Another type of test item asks you to arrange a series of items or events in some order, such as the steps you follow in a science experiment. Here's how you approach such a question:

1. **Read through all the items.**
2. **See whether you can identify the first and last step.**
3. **Think logically how the others should follow in order.**
4. **Arrange in the appropriate order.**

What Kind of Word Do You Need?

One way to prompt your memory on a fill-in-the-blank question is to think of what type of word you need for the blank. Do you need a person's name? An event? A date? A definition or term? You can then cycle your memory through all the applicable names (events, dates, and so on) from the material you studied to see whether any work.

following section). If you're asked to identify the mad monk from Russia, you have to come up with the name Rasputin. No other name will get you points.

Complete those you do know and, if there's no penalty for guessing, guess on any other blanks. Think of possible terms, definitions, concepts, persons, events, or other items that you studied in the days and weeks leading up to the test.

ESSAY QUESTIONS

Probably the most dreaded type of question is the essay question, because you aren't given any answers to choose from and you're faced with a blank page that you need to complete. Keep in mind that this type of question will be used more and more often as your schooling progresses, and your instructor wants to see evidence that you can apply and really understand information (versus memorizing and recalling information).

Don't despair. You can build your confidence in responding to essay questions, and in doing so, improve your performance.

To start, budget time for this type of question if there are other questions on the test. Often, an essay question is the last question on the test and is worth a significant portion of the points. Don't spend all your time on the other questions; make time to both plan and write your essay.

Before you start writing, read the question carefully and note what the essay should include. Then map out a plan of your answer. You might jot down the key points you want to make, and then organize them in order (in order of importance, chronologically, or some other logical order). You can also jot down a mini-outline. When you know the points you want to make, you're better prepared to state your answer directly in the introduction and back it up with examples.

Use direct statements and back up each of your main points of your argument with facts, statistics, and your own opinion from the readings, lectures, and other resources. Include only pertinent information in each paragraph. Don't try to pad it with information that you remember (but that doesn't relate). Also weed out any repetition. You won't get a better grade (and will likely get a worse one) if you add to the length by restating the same idea, using different words.

Keep your paragraphs focused on one idea and use transitions to link one idea to the next. Main paragraphs in a balanced essay are usually equal lengths. Keep this in mind as you write. You don't want to provide an entire page to support one point and then, because of lack of time or material, only mention your other ideas.

As in any writing, use correct grammar and spelling (as well as you can, without a dictionary) and write legibly. Check your work. Look for sentence fragments or run-ons and fix them during your review. Don't get points deducted for easy mistakes that you can correct by proofreading.

Improve Writing Skills

When you improve your writing skills, your essay test skills will also improve. A well-written paper and essay share common goals. Both should state the main idea or argument, provide detailed information to support that argument, and be organized well. Chapter 8 covers effective writing.

Strategies for Test Subjects

Different subjects lend themselves to different types of tests, as mentioned in Chapter 5. Therefore, your preparation will vary, depending on the subject of the test. This section gives you some specific advice on what to expect on particular tests for different subjects.

PREPARING FOR A MATH TEST

Most often, in a math test, you solve problems, such as formulas, equations, word problems, logic questions, and so on. The best way to prepare for a math test is to practice sample problems that are likely to be on the test.

When studying, practice all types of problems, but focus especially on the problems for which you didn't receive full credit in your homework, quizzes, or in-class assignments.

Be sure to check your work. Even if the instructor doesn't require it, show your work on scrap paper so that when you review your answers, you can check each step of the equation from your work.

PREPARING FOR A HISTORY OR SOCIAL STUDIES TEST

History and social studies focus on countries, events, cultures, geography, wars, people, and more. You may be tested on recalling key facts, such as the date an event occurred or the name of a ruler or capital. You may also have to fill in a map or put a series of events in order. When studying, try to choose the most important

Extra Help

If you really struggle with math, consider getting some outside help, such as a tutor (see Chapter 10). Or consider purchasing a book or computer program that reviews and lets you practice a certain math skill or concept on your own.

facts. For recall information, your instructor may include multiple-choice, true-or-false, matching, or fill-in-the blank questions. Review the "Strategies for Typical Test Questions" section for tips on handling these types of questions.

In addition to objective test questions (like true-or-false and matching), your history or social studies instructor may include essay questions. An essay enables your instructor to see how well you made sense of the information and how you can relate the information to other similar events or issues. To prepare for possible essay questions, look for themes that your instructor or textbook stresses or that you notice. If your book includes discussion questions, test yourself using those; your instructor is likely to include similar essay questions on your test.

PREPARING FOR A SCIENCE TEST

When you study science, you need to read and make sense of information about how things work, why something occurs as it does, who discovered key scientific facts, who invented key technology, and more. For this type of knowledge, you need to be able to read and remember the facts when you study.

In addition, you may learn procedural skills, such as what steps to follow when performing an experiment or how to solve mathematical problems that underlie or relate to science. To study for this type of test, practice the applicable skills — for example, solve sample problems.

PREPARING FOR AN ENGLISH
OR LITERATURE TEST

Depending on your grade and school, English and literature (or reading) may be taught in one class or may be taught separately. As you progress through school, you'll find that English grammar and linguistics classes focus on sentence structure, grammar, spelling, vocabulary, *etymology* (language origins), and other similar topics. English classes of this sort focus on English as a language, and you're tested differently than you are for literature and reading classes. For example, on a vocabulary test, you may have a list of definitions and terms and have to match them. Or your instructor may include fill-in-the-blank questions, for which you need to supply the missing term. To test grammar, you may have to edit a paragraph, correcting spelling and grammatical mistakes. English tests, then, require some recall (that is, learning definitions) as well as some practical application (such as correcting grammar). Your approach to studying will be based on the type of test. For recall tests, study the material. For practical tests, practice.

For tests in reading or literature classes, you may be tested on the content to see whether you remember key events, characters, images, and settings in the literature you've read. Your instructor may want to make sure you know the basics of the story. To study for this type of test, do your reading; in your notes, you may also want to write a summary of the novel or make a list of key dates, characters, events, images, places, and so on.

To test how well you understand the novel on a deeper level, your instructor may include essay questions on the test. These questions may ask you to express your own opinions about the story, take a stand on a particular issue raised in the story, relate the story to something else (such as a historical event or a more modern place and time), document the evolution or changes of a character, discuss why characters act a certain way, explain the symbolism used in the story, and describe what the story says about a larger concept (such as love or family), and more.

To prepare for this type of test, make sure you understand the basic facts of the story first. Then use discussion or review questions to delve beyond the basics of the story. Your instructor may lead the class in a discussion of these questions, or you may break into small groups and talk about the ideas on your own. Your instructor may also lecture on the story, providing information about the author or the time in which the piece was written to enable you to better understand the story.

PERFORMANCE TESTS

For some types of subjects, you may actually perform a series of actions as the test. For example, music, physical education, drama, foreign languages, and other classes often require that you show mastery of some skill. In music, you may have to sing or play a song on an instrument. In physical education, you may have to do a certain number of pushups or sit-ups, or you may need to demonstrate the basic techniques of a sport. For drama, you may need to make an oral presentation, such as act a particular role in a play. For speech or debate, you often do research to prepare an oral presentation (somewhat like writing a paper), and then give the speech or participate in a debate. Foreign languages usually require that you not only perform well on written tests but also are able to speak the language.

The best way to prepare for performance-based tests is to practice. For example, if you'll be tested on your ability to make free throws in basketball, practice your free throws. If you need to play a recital piece in music or a role in a stage production, practice playing or acting. To show that you can speak in a foreign language, practice not only your usage, but also the pronunciation of the language, preferably with another person.

OTHER TYPES OF ASSESSMENTS

In addition to tests, your instructor may use other methods to assess your knowledge of different classes. For example, in literature or reading classes, you may write a paper or create some type of presentation (a play or video, for example). In a science class, you may create a science project — do research, conduct an experiment, and present your findings.

Your instructor should give you specific details about any forms of assessment as well as how they relate to your overall grade. Chapter 7 (doing research) and Chapter 8 (writing papers) should also be of help when preparing these types of assessments.

Doing Research

> *The universe is made up of stories, not of atoms.*
>
> —Muriel Rukeyser

Often, in your classes, you need to write a research paper. For example, you may need to do research for a science project, or you may do research about a particular country and its culture for a social studies or history class. You may need to do research on a health issue for your health class. For these and other similar projects, you need to know how to research properly and effectively.

Research isn't limited only to big projects, either. You can do research to quickly locate a fact or to complete a homework assignment. You can also research current events for a debate class. For science, you can bring in a recent article from the news to discuss a recent scientific development in class. So, in addition to major research projects, your instructor may require you to do research for homework and in-class assignments.

Research has become both simpler and more complex. It's simpler (and quicker) because, if you have a computer, you can find information you need by searching the Internet. For all your information, you don't have to trek to the library, use the card catalog, find the resource (and hope no one else has it), find the relevant pages in the resource, and then take notes on the information. Instead, you can find some sources from the Internet. You can use a search tool (such as Google), search the Internet, browse relevant articles from your computer, and then print copies of those of interest. Keep in mind, though, that you usually want to consult a variety of types of sources. That is, you shouldn't always rely just on the Internet for your research.

While finding information is easier than ever, at the same time, researching has become more complex. There's a lot more material available, which means you may be overwhelmed with the amount of information. You need to learn how to sort through and find the relevant information for your particular project. Also, you need to check the accuracy or authenticity of your sites if you reference a Web site. Even famous newscasters can get caught up in the "Web" of information. In 2003, CBS News reported a major story incorrectly; its sources were from the Internet, but the sources were not correct.

This chapter focuses on basic research skills, using typical resources, such as your school library, local library, and the Internet. (Throughout this book, you can find information on improving your study skills by using technology. Chapter 9 provides a more in-depth look, focusing specifically on using technology to help your studies.)

To start, this chapter explains how to select a topic. Choosing a good topic is critical to your success, but often it's the most rushed aspect of a project. In this chapter, you find out how to brainstorm ideas, check the idea to make sure it meets the requirements of the project, and more. In addition, this chapter explains what types of resources you can expect to find at your school library and local library and explains when you may want to use these resources (such as the *Reader's Guide to Periodical Literature*, a list of all magazine articles published on a topic within a certain time period). You also find out how to use the Internet to do research.

When including researched content in your work, don't ever use someone else's words or ideas and claim them as your own. This is one of the potential dangers of doing research; you must cite information that comes from another source. This chapter covers also how to avoid plagiarism and how to accurately document the sources you do use.

Selecting a Topic

One of the most important steps of a research assignment is selecting a topic. You want a topic that is of interest to you, matches the requirements of the assignment, and is relevant to your studies. You also want to be sure that you can find information on your topic of choice. The following sections focus on the first step of starting a research assignment: selecting a topic.

UNDERSTANDING THE ASSIGNMENT

When you're given a research assignment, the instructor usually provides an assignment sheet or other resource that details the requirements of the assignment. For example, she may have you complete a research assignment from your textbook, or he may create his own assignment sheet. The assignment sheet is important because it tells you what the instructor expects as well as other information about putting together the research project (such as formatting information like fonts, margins, and so on). When you know what's expected of you, you are more likely to match those requirements and expectations when doing the assignment. This effort translates to a better grade.

Instead of skimming over the assignment sheet and not paying too much attention to it until after the research assignment is complete and you're just double-checking that you got it right, spend time early reading and thinking about the goals and parts of the assignment. For major research projects, be sure you know the following before you begin:

✓ **Type of assignment:** Instructors often assign research papers as the type of research assignment, but you may also be challenged to create other types of research projects, including presentations, oral reports, posters, videos, group games, and more. A lot of times, instructors require a written component (such as a paper) and an oral component (such as a brief oral report to your class). Know exactly what you need to create to meet the requirements of the assignment.

✓ **Subject of assignment:** Usually, an assignment is based on something you're studying in class. You may take, for example, a more detailed look at a historical event. Or you may focus on a particular country or a time period in history. While the subject isn't the same as your topic, the subject does provide the basic arena for the assignment and is a starting point for coming up with a topic for the assignment.

✓ **Length of assignment:** Your instructor should give you some idea of the expected length of the assignment. For reports, this may be a certain number of pages or words. For oral presentations, this may be a certain number of minutes to make the presentation. The length is important because it's a criterion you use to select the topic. For example, if the goal is to write a 4- to 6-page paper, the topic of World War II is too big. Women's role in that war, though, is a more focused the topic for a paper of that length.

✓ **Expected resources:** Your instructor will probably provide some ideas about where you can find information to complete the assignment. She may even require you to use a particular source, such as a recent news article or an Internet site. The expected resources can tell you the type of information your instructor expects to see in the research assignment.

✓ **Elements:** Your instructor should also specify any special elements the report should include. For example, your instructor may ask that you include an outline of your paper. Or you may need to show graphs or charts of your experiments for a science report. As another example, your instructor may want you to include illustrations or relevant photographs to enhance your report. In addition to the body of the research assignment, know what other items the instructor expects in your final report. You can then look for these elements when you're doing your research.

✓ **Format:** The instructor should also provide you with detailed instructions on how the research assignment should look. For papers, this may include the typeface, font size, margins, title page, and other formatting elements such as headers and footers. For presentations, you may need to create a slide

Note Your Resources during Research

The time to record citation information is as you're doing your research. If you wait until the end, when you're creating a Works Cited page, you may find that you're missing information. You'll then have to take the time to locate the resource again and write down the required details, such as the publisher or place of publication or page numbers used.

presentation (using programs such as PowerPoint), create a movie using a video camera, provide note cards for your oral report, and so on. The format should tell you exactly what your research assignment should look like when you turn it in or present it.

✓ **Citations:** When you include someone else's words or ideas, always cite the source. You can use different methods for citations. You may include footnotes, *endnotes* (which are like footnotes but they appear at the end of the document on a separate page), or in-text citations (which appear in parenthesis, following the cited material). You need to not only know how to cite the information but also understand in what format you should list the works you cited (called a *Works Cited page* or *Bibliography*). The "Citing Sources" section later in this chapter covers the topic of citations in more detail.

When you know the expectations of the assignment, you're ready to select your topic, as covered in the following section.

GETTING IDEAS FOR TOPICS

Research assignments often require a lot of time and may count for a significant part of your grade. Therefore, you should start by selecting a topic that is of interest to you and relevant to the assignment. Doing so improves your chances of getting a better grade.

To come up with possible topics, you can use many sources. Rather than selecting the first topic that comes to mind, consider making a list of potential topics, evaluating each one, and then making a decision.

For potential research assignment topics, consider these possible sources or methods for generation topics:

✓ **Ask your instructor.** Your instructor may provide some sample topics. You may want to choose one of these, or you might be able to use these as a way to brainstorm additional ideas. If your instructor doesn't specifically provide any possible topics, you can ask for some, especially if you're having a difficult time coming up with a topic. As another alternative, sometimes the instructor provides all of the topics, and you *must* select from the list.

✓ **Review your textbook and other class materials.** Look through your textbook or other course materials, because they may include sample research assignment topics or projects. You can select one of the ones mentioned, or you can use the recommendations as a starting point to brainstorm new ideas.

✓ **Brainstorm ideas.** To brainstorm a possible topic, start with a word or phrase that describes the general subject (World War II, for example, or biology). With the subject in mind, list any ideas that you can think of. Don't worry about whether

Assigned Topics

If you're really unhappy with an assigned topic, ask for something different. Have some valid reasons why the current topic doesn't interest you (instead of saying, "I just don't like it"). Also, present the instructor with some possible topics that are of interest to you and that meet the requirements of the assignment. He or she may let you change.

Brainstorm in Groups

If you're stuck, ask someone else to help you brainstorm ideas. You may ask your classmates, friends, siblings, or parents to help you come up with ideas.

the topic is perfect and don't judge your brainstormed list of entries as you create it. Just list as many ideas as you can think of. Later, you can weed out the topics that don't work. Sometimes, a weird idea leads to a new, appropriate idea, so note all your ideas without editing.

To brainstorm, ask yourself several questions. What do you know about the subject? What have you read about the subject? Has the subject been in the news recently? If so, why? What would you like to learn about the subject? What questions do you have about the subject? What's related to this subject that's of interest to you?

✓ **Check out printed materials.** Look through your school or local library and see what books or articles are available on the subject. Think about what books, articles, or other information you have read about the general subject. For example, you may have read a novel or seen a TV show about da Vinci's paintings that aroused questions that you can answer in a research paper.

✓ **Use the Internet.** In addition to printed materials, you can use the Internet to search for general information, which can then help you brainstorm specific ideas. For example, you may be interested in Pearl Harbor (as part of your World War II studies). Search for Pearl Harbor and see what type of information is available. From that information, you may be able to come up with a relevant, focused topic, such as why Pearl Harbor was vulnerable, how the bombing affected the U.S. involvement or the history of the state. To get other ideas, you may also search generically for examples of different projects, such as "science fair projects" and review any matching examples.

EVALUATING YOUR TOPIC

After you generate a list of potential topics, you can evaluate each one, selecting the one that's the best match for your interests and the particulars of the assignment. Ask yourself the following questions about the possible topic(s):

- ✓ **Is the topic interesting?** If the topic isn't interesting to you, it's not likely to be of interest to your audience (even if your "audience" is just your instructor). Also, you won't be as enthused as you research and complete the assignment if you aren't interested. To make your research assignment more enjoyable (and the outcome better), choose a topic that you find intriguing.

- ✓ **Is the topic relevant to what you're studying?** For example, if you're studying rain forests, your instructor isn't likely to allow you to do your research assignment on the Great Wall of China. Make sure the topic relates to the goal and subject of the assignment.

- ✓ **Is the scope manageable?** If you choose an assignment that's difficult to research, you may have trouble coming up with enough content. On the other hand, if you choose a topic that's too broad, you may have too much material. You want just the right scope. You also want to be sure that the information you need is available (from your school library, local library, the Internet, or other resources).

- ✓ **Will you be able to meet the goals of the assignment with this topic?** If the goal is to research a topic and conduct a scientific experiment, a topic such as Devil's Triangle (an area in the Atlantic Ocean where planes have been thought to disappear; also called the Bermuda Triangle), while interesting, won't work because you don't have an experiment that can feasibly prove or disprove your theories.

Not Sure about the Assignment?

If you aren't sure whether your topic is a good fit for the assignment, ask your instructor. Most often, instructors are happy to provide feedback on a topic. Your instructor may give you suggestions for narrowing or broadening the scope as well as suggest possible resources for the assignment.

Understanding Types of Research Materials

Armed with a topic, you can begin your quest for gathering information for the assignment. Before you head off to the library or hook up to the Internet, consider first the various types of materials that are commonly used in research assignments. Doing so can help you determine not only what types of information you seek but also the pros and cons of each type. You can also discover where you can find these sources (see the "Finding Resources" section). The following sections cover the general materials you commonly use in a research assignment.

REFERENCE BOOKS

When you want to quickly look up a fact or statistic, turn to reference books. These types of books include atlases, encyclopedias, dictionaries (including special dictionaries for medicine, physics, computers, and other special fields), almanacs, maps, biographical dictionaries (such as *Who's Who in America* or *Dictionary of American Biography*), government guides, yearbooks (not your school yearbook, but formal yearbooks that include information about what happened during a particular year, including statistical information, miscellaneous facts, and summary of key events), and other similar resources.

This type of book can give you a good overview of a topic and may provide some useful facts and statistics, but you often have to go beyond just the general picture presented in a reference book. As another drawback, reference books may not include the most recent information. For example, an encyclopedia may not be published frequently enough to cover new trends or topics.

So that they are available to everyone, reference books cannot be checked out of a library. You must review the information (and take notes or copy the materials) in the library. You can also find some reference material on the Internet.

REGULAR BOOKS

In addition to reference books, you may consult other books for information on your topic. You may find entire books or just portions of books devoted to your topic. Books are often useful for getting a more in-depth look at a topic. Also, books may show how the topic relates to other topics and issues (versus a reference entry that's independent and focused on only the topic).

Unlike reference books, you can check books out of a library. On the downside, if someone has already checked out the book you need, you may have to go to another library or find another resource.

MAGAZINES, JOURNALS, AND ARTICLES FROM OTHER SOURCES

For current information on your topic, you may consult recent magazines, journals, newspapers, and other printed materials. For

Special Collections

Libraries also often have special collections that may include rare books. (You usually need permission to access and review these materials.) You can also find tapes, videos, CDs, DVDs, and other materials.

Use an Abstract Index

An abstract index functions like a periodical guide, only it summarizes information in the article (referred to as an *abstract*). You can also use these collections to not only find relevant articles but also read a summary (rather than track them down in the library) to see whether they are worth reviewing. You can find these indexes in your library.

---

example, you may read about a new breakthrough in cancer research in a magazine or newspaper. To find what's been recently published in these resources, you use a guide that lists recent (and older) articles and their specific publication information. For example, one popular guide is the *Reader's Guide to Periodical Literature,* a reference you can find at the library. You can also find other guides, including the *MLA International Bibliography.*

The *Readers' Guide to Periodical Literature* categorizes articles by topic, and then includes the relevant articles and publication information for those articles. You then use the publication information to find that article; see the "Finding a Magazine Article" section later in this chapter.

Articles provide timely, up-to-date information. On the other hand, you can't always tell from the information in the index whether the article contains information useful for your assignment. You usually have to read the actual article to see whether it's relevant. Also, finding the actual articles can be difficult. Not all libraries carry or keep all periodicals.

You can also find newspaper articles, also by using an index. Not all newspapers have indexes, but you can find indexes for popular, big papers such as *The New York Times* (and its index).

WEB SITE RESOURCES

In addition to printed resources, you can also find resources online. You may be able to find recent statistics or facts from reference sites, such as government sites like the Bureau of Labor and Statistics (www.bls.gov). You may also find articles posted online about a particular topic. (See the "Using Internet Resources" section for more information.) Web site information is usually current, and searching the Internet is fast and convenient. You don't have to worry about someone else checking out the resource you need.

The drawbacks include information overload and issues with accuracy.

✓ **Information overload:** When you search for a topic, you may be overwhelmed with the results. You'll have to sort through the first several pages of matches and determine which sites and articles are relevant.

✓ **Accuracy:** Check to see who has written or posted the article and/or who's in charge of the site. For the most part, anyone can create his or her own Web site and post any information, whether it's true or not. You need to make sure the author and/or site is reputable. You can do so by checking out the credentials of the author (if he or she is listed) or the site (look for a link called About this Site or something similarly named).

Finding Resources

Now that you know what types of resources are available, you can set off on your information hunt. You may want to sketch out your "ideal" list of information. What information would you like to find? What information do you need to include? What information

---

Search Newspaper Archives

Most newspapers enable you to search recent publications online without a fee. If you want access to archives, though, you may be required to pay a fee to access the complete set of archives for past dates.

Books and Accuracy

Because a printed book goes through many different hands and editorial processes, you can most often trust its information if it has been published by a reputable publisher. The publisher usually has checked the author's credentials, and the book has been through an editorial process, through which several different types of editors have reviewed and commented on the manuscript. Because of this process, you can usually trust the contents of published books over other media.

would help you complete the assignment? If you know what you're looking for, it's easier to find it.

Your instructor may give you guidelines, for example, on what information you need to include. You might have a list of facts or issues that you need to include in the assignment. For example, if you're doing a report on a country, your instructor may require that you include the most recent population information, a map of the country, information about culture, and so on. Use this list, if you have one, as a guide for finding the information.

Your research should be a combination of browsing to see what's available and to find new information, as well as searching to find specific information. This section covers how to find information, both browsing and searching, using various resources.

USING YOUR CLASSROOM MATERIALS

One resource that you may overlook that is often the best starting place for a research assignment is your class materials. Your textbook (or other resource) may include ideas for research assignments. Also, your textbook may include specific information that's useful for your report, such as facts, maps, statistics, lists, illustrations, charts, and so on. If your textbook is helpful, you can use its information in your research assignment. And finally, and maybe

Think Specifically

When you're doing research, it's much easier if you specifically list or know what information you need. For example, it's much easier to search for "population of Italy" than it is to search for "Italy," and then wade through all the various matches to find that piece of information. Consider making a list of all the key items you need to find and include in your research assignment.

most importantly, your textbook often lists other relevant resources. You may find these resources listed at the end of each chapter, in footnotes, in an appendix of the textbook, or within the material itself. Therefore, review your textbook, noting any information you may want to include and listing any possible other resources you may consult in your research.

FINDING SOURCES AT A LIBRARY

After reviewing your textbook, your next stop is commonly the library. You may visit the school or university library or your local library. At the library, you can use reference books as well as find and check out books.

In older libraries that have not upgraded to computerized systems, you'll find long drawers of cards, and you look up the book by going to the appropriate section (by article, subject, or keyword), and then looking through the cards, which are arranged alphabetically. With computerized systems, you can type in the author, title, subject, or search by keyword to find available works. The search displays matches, which you can review to select possible resources to track down and potentially include in your research assignment.

The card catalog (physical or its computer counterpart) provides you with the call letter of the book, and this call letter or number tells you where the book is stored. Different libraries use different systems. The original library system was the Dewey Decimal. In this system, all topics fall in the range from 0 to 1,000, but this large range is broken down by subject. For example, literature books are numbered with numbers within the 800–899 range. That category is further broken down into subtopics, with each number assigned a particular topic. For example, drama works have a call number of 822. Decimals are added to even further categorize the work, so you may start with a call number such as 822.3.

The Library of Congress uses a different system. It contains 21 broad categories, each assigned a letter. A second letter is added to specify the subcategory within the main category (for example, PS). A specific number range further classifies and identifies the specific book.

You can also find magazine articles (covered in the following section), use their computers to access the Internet, and browse through other materials at the library. Check with your librarian for specific directions on using their library system as well as any other features (Internet access, for example).

Finding Magazine Articles

To find current information, be sure to review recent articles in magazines, journals, and other publications that are published frequently. The collection of magazines, journals, and other publications is

Benefits of Computerized Catalogs

Not only is computerized searching quick and flexible (enabling you to search on keywords and combine search criteria), but it also gives you the status of the work (whether it's checked out, in the library, not available, not available at this branch but available at another branch, and so on). This saves you from having to look through the library for a book that's not there.

Popular Reference Books

Beyond the examples mentioned already in this chapter, you may consider looking at the following reference works: *World Almanac* and *Book of Facts, Information Please Almanac, The Statesman's Yearbook* (facts about world government), and the *Statistical Abstract of the U.S.*

known as *periodicals,* and the resource you use to see whether any articles have appeared in print on your topic, you can use the *Reader's Guide to Periodical Literature* or other similar guide that collates, combines, and categorizes articles printed in magazines and journals.

These books are most often housed in the reference section of the library and are published in volumes. During the current year, you usually find issues that deal with a set time period (like the first quarter or a particular month, depending on the index). At the end of the year, all of the months are published in one volume. Therefore, to look for articles that appeared in 2002, you'd use the 2002 Volume. To look for articles published in the current year, you'd use one (or several) of the volumes (mini-compilations) for that year.

To use a guide such as the *Reader's Guide to Periodical Literature,* follow these steps:

1. **Look up the research topic.** The guide lists any articles that have been published on that topic as well as publication information.

2. **Note the specific publication information,** including the name of the periodical (think magazine or journal), volume or issue, page numbers, article title, and author.

3. **With this specific information for the article(s), go to the periodical section of the library and find the specific magazine issue that contains the article.** The periodicals are usually stored in a separate section from books, and you'll find

current issues in magazine bins. Past issues are often bound and stored on the shelves or on microfiche. You may have to ask the librarian to help locate the article. You may also need help learning how to set up and use the microfiche for articles that have been photographed and put on film; again, ask the librarian.

4. **Take notes from the article or copy the article so that you can take it home with you.** Also be sure to note the complete information for the article for your works cited list. (Basically, you need to note the magazine's name, volume or issue, page number, publication date, article title, and author of the article.)

USING INTERNET RESOURCES

The Internet has vastly changed the way you can access information. If you have a computer and an Internet connection, you can browse and search for information on just about every subject conceivable. Consider these suggestions when using the Internet to find information:

✓ **To look up general information, you may want to access a reference source.** You can find online versions of dictionaries, atlases, encyclopedias, and more. You can, for example, use the Internet to look up the climate of Italy or to find and

Check for Magazines

Your library should have a list of periodicals available at that branch (as well as possibly the date ranges that are available for each periodical). Because the guide lists *all* articles, not just those in that library, you may want to familiarize yourself with this list, at least briefly, so that you can look specifically for articles within periodicals you know your library has on hand.

download a copy of the "Sunflowers" to include in a report on Van Gogh.

✓ **To search for specific information, use one of the available search tools.** Popular tools include Yahoo!, Google, and others. You type in a word or phrase, and the search tool displays a list of relevant sites. Your search results usually turn up a variety of information, from articles posted by experts to opinions posted by regular Joes on Web logs *(blogs)*. You'll also find links to news stories, images, and more. Chapter 9 covers searching in more detail and also provides tips on how to most effectively search.

✓ **To see what types of information are available, browse through the search site's links or try the reference tools.** For example, you can browse through categories related to finance or science or today's headlines. You may also find links to maps, weather, and reference tools like dictionaries and the Yellow Pages.

✓ **To locate an image or news article, use a search site that enables you to specifically search for this type of information.** Google, for example, has special tabs. You can click the Image tab, and then search only for images on your topic.

Web Sites for Popular Search Sites

To search, go to the search site. From its start page, you can then access any of the links on that page or search. Currently, the most popular search tool is Google (www.google.com), but other search tools are available such as Yahoo! (www.yahoo.com), AltaVista (www.altavista.com), and others. Different search tools come up with different matches, so it's worth using more than one when you're looking for information.

Suppose you need a picture of the great white shark for a report on sea life; you could use Google's image tool to quickly find an image.

Using Other Resources

In addition to school resources, libraries, and the Internet, you may find other worthwhile resources to include. For example, you may have literature or artistic resources (novels, artwork, plays, memoirs, illustrations) that are worth considering. So, if you are doing a report on Ireland and have read Frank McCourt's *Angela's Ashes,* you may be able to portray a more intimate look by including some details from that popular memoir.

Another possible resource is people who have some experience with the topic. You can conduct interviews to hear and incorporate their ideas. For example, suppose one of your parents works at a popular drug manufacturer. If you do a report on how a drug becomes approved by the FDA, your parent may be able to hook you up to someone who's an expert on this topic. If your parent is an attorney, he or she could explain how the legal system works. If your grandfather, aunt, or uncle served in a war, he or she can give you firsthand accounts of what it was like. Interviews help personalize a topic and make it more captivating.

Also, don't forget one of the most crucial elements of a successful research assignment: your own thoughts and opinions. Students often don't include their own experiences, but that's what transforms a recitation of facts into a more compelling and personal topic. Suppose that in health class you're talking about teenagers and their weight. You may have a friend or relative who has suffered from an eating disorder. You may show firsthand how devastating this problem can be. Instructors will expect you, especially as your education continues, to provide more and more of your insight. Value your own ideas, backing them up with specific examples and showing the information as it affects real life.

Working with Resources

Tracking down the resources you need is probably the most difficult process of the research assignment. You often feel like you are on a scavenger hunt. In your search, you may hit some dead ends: Either the information is not available (for whatever reason) or the information isn't pertinent to your plans for the research assignment.

After you've collected all of the information, though, you can start reviewing it, taking notes, and figuring out the best way to incorporate it into your research assignment. This section covers how to do these things, as well as how to handle citing information from your source.

DECIDING WHAT TO INCLUDE

When you review the various information you have collected, your first decision is what's worth including and what's not. Deciding what to include varies depending on what plan you use to create the research assignment.

Some people like to come up with an outline of the project. Usually, they list the main points they want to make (as well as any subpoints, depending on the detail of the outline). They then match the information they've found to the predefined outline. If the outline has gaps, the researcher can go back and find information to fill in the holes, or he may choose to adapt the outline.

Both methods for deciding how to organize the material require some compromises. For a preset outline, the researcher, for example, may find that she needs to rearrange the order of her points. She may find other relevant points that she uncovered in her research and that fit in the assignment (but weren't in the outline). Another researcher may delete outline topics he planned on including, deciding that they really weren't relevant.

The other method to approach selecting and organizing content is to see what the research itself contains. With this approach, you find the facts and details that are most interesting, and then build your paper about what you find in your research. You may list the main ideas, and then use this list to plan the order of how you present the material. You may create an organized outline about what order you want to present this information.

Taking Out the Fat

Students often think "more is better" when writing a research assignment. They may include just about everything they can find on the topic. This isn't the best approach; you want to focus on and stick to a narrowly defined topic. Delete any extraneous information and instead select only the information that supports your paper.

Repeating the same information over and over is a strategy for increasing length in a research assignment, so it's frowned upon. It's unlikely your instructor won't notice the repetition, no matter how many unique ways you say the same idea only in different words, so avoid repetition.

Like the first method, expect to make compromises. When you arrange the content as determined by what you found, you may find there are gaps. For example, suppose you have facts only about one side of a controversial issue. You should cover both to present a balanced view. Also, you may find information that you really, really like, but doesn't really fit with the goals or requirements of the assignment. You may have to leave out information, even if you like it, if it doesn't serve the purpose of the assignment.

TAKING NOTES

When you review your materials, you can take notes of the most important points. Chapter 4 covers how to take notes, and Chapter 8 focuses specifically on taking notes and keeping track of sources for a research paper. Use this chapter for a practical and organized approach to use.

Keep in mind that in your notes, you want to indicate when you're quoting from the source exactly. Put quotations around the text that is word-by-word from the source. Also use some notation to indicate material that's from the source but has been *paraphrased* (put into your own words). Your notes may also include your own ideas or thoughts as you reviewed the information. (These do not have to be cited.)

To avoid a lot of copying (and forgetting either the publication details of the source or whether something is a direct quote or a paraphrased passage or your own words), you may simply want to photocopy the articles, book pages, reference pages, and other sources. This allows you to refer to them when needed.

Avoiding Plagiarism

Plagiarism is when you take someone else's words or ideas and present them as your own. That's why you need to be careful when doing research, making sure you note what you have quoted directly from a source (magazine article, Web site, reference book, and so on). It's not that you can't include this information from the source — you can. It's only that you have to cite the information. Basically, flagging the information alerts your reader that this isn't your idea but is from another person and source.

Often students worry that citing information means they are relying on others' opinions rather than their own. While a good paper has a mix of both, you shouldn't avoid referencing material just because you want it to appear as if you don't have any original ideas.

Citing sources not only prevents cheating (which plagiarism is) but also shows that the facts you present are backed up by experts and other professionals in that subject.

Citing Sources

Depending on your instructor, you may follow a different set of guidelines. Popular styles include the MLA (Modern Language Association) guidelines and APA Style guide. (MLA is most often used in schools. You can find out information at the MLA site. The address is www.mla.org.) These determine how you cite both direct quotations as well as paraphrased information. For example, in MLA style, you include the author's name and page number in parentheses at the end of the passage that's quoted directly or summarized. Here's an example:

"By then I knew that everything good and bad left emptiness when it stopped. But if it was bad, the emptiness filled up by itself" (Hemingway 62). Your instructor may instruct you to use another citation method, such as footnotes or endnotes, so use the specific guidelines required by the assignment.

In addition to citing the sources as you include them in your research assignment, you also create a Works Cited list or bibliography. Again, this has to be formatted in a specific way and include specific information. This varies depending on the specific citation style preferred by your instructor as well as the type of source. For example, magazine articles include different information than a book, so you need to follow the precise guidelines for the style you are supposed to follow as well as the type of source.

Creating a Works Cited page can be challenging because you need to separate different items using periods, commas, and semi-colons. Don't worry if you can't memorize these or if you don't know off the top of your head how to format them. Most students refer to a reference to remind them of the exact format to use. Get a good resource (one recommended by your instructor) that explains how to cite sources and create a Works Cited page.

Writing Papers

Wonder, not doubt, is the source of all knowledge.

—A.J. Heschel

Most students don't like writing. Why? Many don't know how to start and are afraid of the infamous blank page. Others think that some people are writers and some aren't (and they put themselves in the latter category). Some say, "I'm not going to be a writer, so why should I bother?" And finally, lots of students think that they should be able to just sit down and write a paper in one draft, and when this isn't possible, they get frustrated.

This chapter debunks these myths. First, if you have a plan for writing a paper (see the "Steps for Writing a Paper" section), the blank page will no longer intimidate you. Second, if you can talk, you can write; writing is telling a story on paper, and everyone can do it. Third, writing is a skill that's critical in every kind of business and career. And finally, writing involves several steps, and after you understand that you don't just sit down and crank out a paper, but instead, break up the process into manageable steps, writing becomes easier.

Everyone can improve his or her writing skills. This chapter defines the criteria for a well-written paper, explains the steps to complete a paper, and provides advice on how you can improve your writing skills.

Understanding the Paper-Writing Process

While you may think papers are assigned only in English class, many courses require written reports. Perhaps you need to complete a research paper for a history class. Or you may look into new developments in science, writing a paper, for example, on DNA and crime solutions. In geography, you may complete an analysis of a particular country. And yes, in English, you may be asked to review a work and its key themes.

To start, then, the following sections take a look at the different types of writing projects, the steps for completing a paper, and the criteria that define a well-written paper.

KINDS OF PAPERS

In your academic career, you'll likely be asked to write different types of papers. Most often, your instructor will provide a detailed assignment, explaining the expectations for the assignment. Depending on the goal of the assignment, you may be asked to do any of the following:

- ✓ **Summarize information.** The most basic type of writing assignment is simply a summary of information. You may, for example, need to summarize the events that led to the Civil War.

- ✓ **Describe a process.** You may be asked to describe the steps for something. For example, you may have to write a paper explaining how to set up a Web site.

- ✓ **Review a work.** For reading assignments, you may be asked to critique the work, giving your opinion and backing that up with evidence. For example, you may write a review of *Tom Sawyer*.

- ✓ **Compare and contrast different items.** Some assignments require you *compare* (describe what they have in common) and *contrast* (describe what's different) two items. For example, you can compare and contrast two characters in a play.

> ## Argue!
>
> Really, all of your papers should have some element of argument. Without an argumentative edge, a paper can turn out to be just a summary of what others have said. Your goal is to say something new and different.

Or you can compare and contrast two approaches to a problem.

✓ **Argue a point.** Some assignments ask you to find a controversy or problem, choose a side, and then present arguments to support your point of view. For example, you may be asked to argue for or against the death penalty.

PARTS OF A TYPICAL PAPER

Even though there are different types of papers, most share a typical structure or organization and include the same elements. In particular, expect to include an opening paragraph (including a thesis statement), the body of the paper, any graphical elements, and a summary.

The opening paragraph should capture your reader's interest and present your thesis statement. The *thesis statement* is your opinion; that is, the argument you intend to make in the paper. In addition to identifying this element, the thesis statement outlines the reasons for your opinion.

The bulk of the paper is the called the *body*. Here's where you support the main idea you presented in the opening. The body text is broken up into paragraphs, and each paragraph should be centered on one key idea.

Some reports include graphic elements such as figures, illustrations, pictures, or tables. As the saying goes, "A picture is worth a thousand words." A picture can present the data in a snapshot to the reader.

Finally, the paper ends with a summary. The least imaginative summary simply restates the argument. It's better, though, to end with a bang. Ask yourself, "What does the information you presented mean to the reader? How can the reader use this information in his or her own experiences? What's next?" Use your answers to compose an exciting summary.

WHAT MAKES A SUCCESSFUL PAPER

Including the various elements in the right order won't necessarily net you a good grade on your paper. And if you just present information that someone else has said, the paper will be mediocre at best. Instead, make a creative statement that's backed up with evidence. A successful paper includes these features:

✓ **An interesting topic:** You find out more about choosing a topic in the "Picking a Topic" section later in this chapter.

✓ **A unique thesis statement:** This is probably the hardest element to master; you may struggle with moving from what someone else has said to summarizing your own opinion.

✓ **Thoughtful and organized content:** Not only do you need to provide adequate information to make your points, but these ideas need to be organized in a logical manner. You can use

Ugh! Grammar

Most students associate writing with following every grammar rule. They see writing as a strict, dull, red-pencil, threatening task. While good grammar is an integral part of good writing, it's not the only element. Think of it as a game. When you play baseball, you have to know what you can and cannot do. After you master the rules, you're free to enjoy the game! The same is true for writing. After you master some basic grammar rules, you can then concentrate on *what* you want to say versus *how* you say it.

the "Organizing Your Paper" section for help on achieving this goal.

✓ **The proper format:** This includes not only following the instructions your instructor gave you but also making sure the document doesn't include any spelling or grammatical errors. Turn to the "Revising Your Writing" section for more information on this element.

STEPS FOR WRITING A PAPER

Now that you know the different elements and criteria for a well-written assignment, take a look at the four basic steps you follow to create any type of paper.

1. **Identify your topic.** This step not only includes choosing a topic but also involves thinking about what you want to say about that topic.

2. **Gather your information.** This means finding resources, doing research, and taking notes.

3. **Write the paper.** This step includes organizing your thoughts and getting them down.

4. **Revise and proof the paper.** Even the best authors revise their work, and revision doesn't just mean checking for grammar or spelling errors (although this is important). You should also read your work, checking for missing information, awkward wording, and poor organization. The "Reviewing an Editing Checklist" section near the end of this chapter includes a checklist for reviewing your work.

Picking a Topic

The first step in writing a paper is choosing a topic, and your paper will be doomed from the start without a good topic. This may sound melodramatic, but it's true. You want to get off to a good start, and this means spending some time deciding on your topic. This section defines what instructors mean by a "good" topic and also explains how you can come up with interesting topics for your papers.

IS THE TOPIC INTERESTING?

To start, a good topic should be of interest to you. If you don't care about the topic, you can't expect your readers to. You'll be more motivated to do your research and really think about your topic if you choose something that's relevant to you. You may, for example, focus on your favorite author, country, hobby, and so on.

You can also select a topic that's relevant to your family, your hometown, or your goals in life. For example, suppose that you want to be a TV weather forecaster. You can look for weather-related aspects of a topic, such as how weather affected certain battles in World War II. Or you can compare and contrast how weather affects people's outlook on life; are people happier when it's sunny most of the time?

IS THE INFORMATION AVAILABLE?

When considering a topic, you also want to make sure you can find the information you need to adequately discuss this topic. (In some cases, you won't find out there's a problem until you do the research.) If you want to write about how Kurt Cobain's journal writing predicted his tragic life, you need access to those journals. Part of choosing a topic is making sure you can find enough sources that discuss it.

IS THE TOPIC THE RIGHT SIZE?

This may sound funny, but the scope of your paper needs to be the right size. That is, your topic can't be too big or too small. Like Goldilocks in "The Three Bears," the topic must be "just right."

When you do your research, you can get a good idea of the scope of your topic by looking at what's available. If there's an overabundance of material, your topic is probably too big. For example, it would be hard to summarize the history of rock and roll in a three-page paper. On the other hand, writing about the use of the sitar (an instrument) in rock and roll probably isn't big enough. Writing about Eastern musical influences on rock, though, may be just right.

How to Find the Right Topic

You know the criteria for a good topic, but how do you come up with one? Consider any of the following:

- ✓ **Look to see what's already been done.** You'll find there's some overlap between choosing a topic and doing your research. You can start with a general idea, and then see how it has been discussed, and that prompts more of your own ideas.

- ✓ **Brainstorm.** Write down any words or phrases that remind you of the topic. Ask your friends or family for their thoughts. Collect as many ideas as possible so that you can make a good selection.

- ✓ **Ask your instructor.** Your instructor may have to approve a topic before you start the assignment. Even if topic approval isn't required, you can still ask your instructor whether he thinks a topic is suitable. Your instructor is also a good resource for possible research sources, the topic of the following section.

Researching Your Work

Choosing a topic is the first step. Next, you need to see what research is available on that topic. Chapter 7 covers research in

Search the Internet

If you have a general topic, search the Internet, and then review the different types of pages, articles, and resources you find.

No Censoring!

When you brainstorm, don't censor your ideas. Just let them go, even if they sound silly. Sometimes, a silly idea eventually leads to a good topic.

more detail; in the following sections, you get some advice on research as it relates to writing a paper.

KNOWING IN ADVANCE WHAT YOU WANT TO FIND

Before you start hitting the library or the Internet, spend some time thinking about what you hope to find. If a magic genie appeared on your desk and said, "What do you need to complete this paper?", what would you say? What information do you need to make your arguments? Jot down any ideas you have. This wish list will give you some direction when you start your hunt for information.

KNOW WHAT YOUR AUDIENCE EXPECTS

Picture your audience. To whom are you writing? What are their characteristics? What convinces them? Moves them? Angers them? It's easy to just think of a general audience or to write for the instructor alone, but doing so can make the paper too generic,

Imagine

A well-designed writing assignment provides a clear audience. Even if the assignment doesn't include a stated audience, you still want to imagine one.

too bland. Instead, think about your paper as an article, and then ask, "Where would I publish it? Who would read it?"

The whole paper process is kind of contrived, because you're writing for the instructor. Still, you'll improve your writing skills if you think of a more specific audience. You'll also be able to find and evaluate your research if you think about your readers' needs.

FINDING SOURCES

Now that you have a good plan for what you're looking for, you can set off on your hunt. In doing your research, consider books, magazines and newspapers, the Internet, and other media.

You can search for relevant books at your library. As another option, consider online sources of books, such as Amazon.com, which enables you to display sample pages from some books. You can use this to look at tables of contents, back covers, sample pages, or other parts of books. Using this preview, you can get a sense of the book's content. Does it contain information you need? You may then decide to track it down at your library.

For some Amazon.com titles, you can even search through a book. For example, suppose you find a title that sounded interesting, but you aren't sure whether it's relevant to your idea. If the book is available for searching on Amazon.com, you can find out.

Other sources of information include magazines and newspapers. Your library should have current magazines and newspapers, as well as access to past issues. You can see whether any magazines or newspapers cover a topic using online search tools or the *Reader's Guide to Periodical Literature*. (Chapter 7 covers periodical research in more detail.)

> ## Recommended Reading
>
> If you find a good book, check the recommended reading or bibliography for that book. This can help you locate other potential sources of information.

It's Good to Disagree

Look for sources that disagree with your argument so that you can identify various viewpoints. If you include sources that cover only your point of view, your paper won't offer a fair, balanced argument.

The Internet is also a rich source of material; it has revolutionized how you do research (among other things). You may be able to find all you need without leaving your home.

Finally, consider other types of media, including movies, documentaries, illustrations, fictional work, and so on.

TAKING NOTES ON YOUR RESEARCH

When you do your research, you can take notes, make copies of pertinent information, and/or print data from the Internet. When you're including information from another source, a little organization goes a long way. Because you need to cite any information you take verbatim or paraphrase, make sure any such information is connected to a source and that you have complete bibliographical information on that source.

Many instructors suggest an index-card method for taking notes and tracking sources. Basically, you complete an index card for each source (with complete information), and then label each source (A, B, C, for example). You then use those cards to write out your research. At the top of the card, you can indicate which source by including its label (A, B, C). Index cards are also useful in organizing the paper's content (covered in the "Organizing Your Paper" section).

You may prefer a different method. For example, you may use legal pads and pens. (If you write on paper, don't write on both sides. You'll see why in the "Organizing Your Paper" section.) Or if you have a computer, you may want to type your research directly; this saves your having to retype the research you wrote out by hand. Use whatever method is most comfortable for you.

Citing Your Sources

When you're including someone else's idea, credit that person. Taking another person's ideas and presenting them as your own is known as *plagiarism,* and you not only can get an F for plagiarizing, but you may also be disciplined in some other way (fail the course, for example) or even expelled from school. Most people know to cite text that they have copied exactly from a source, but you also should cite places in which you paraphrase someone's ideas. (You *paraphrase* when you read someone else's opinion and restate it in your own words.)

Note that you don't have to cite historical or scientific facts.

Organizing Your Paper

Now you probably have a collection of information either on index cards, legal pads, or in a word processing document. What's next? You may think it's time to sit down to write, but that's like setting off on a road trip without a map. (Sure, wandering is okay for some road trips, but it won't fly for your writing requirements.) Organizing helps you think about what you want to write. It also ensures that you cover all of your points. And when you do start writing,

Check Your Sources

If you include text verbatim from a source, copy carefully and put quote marks around all copied material. If you paraphrase, make sure you indicate that the material isn't yours. You do this by citing it in footnotes, endnotes, a bibliography, or a Works Cited page. See the "Citing Your Sources" section.

Use an Outline

Most word processing programs have an outline feature that lets you create a numbered outline. In Microsoft Word, for instance, you simply change to Outline view and use the Tab key to indicate the level of each heading. You can use this to develop your organizational structure for your paper.

you can concentrate on that (the writing) instead of on the order of the information.

So how do you organize? Well, your research provides the basis for your organization. Ask yourself, "What did I learn? What do I want to say?"

You can play around with the ideas by arranging your research. For example, if you have index cards, you can create piles for similar ideas, each one making one main point. After you divvy up the information, you can then organize the piles into a logical order.

If you wrote on paper, you can cut up the paper into ideas and do the same sorting as for index cards. (That's why you don't want to write on the back of any page.) If you typed your research, you can rearrange your ideas using the Cut and Paste commands in your word processing program.

If you're having trouble logically arranging your outline, you can think of some typical paper organizations to see whether one would work. Consider any of the following.

✓ **Timeline or chronological order:** This organization structure makes sense if time is an element of the topic (or story). You should, though, avoid saying, "and then, and then, and then." (Think about that scene at the Chinese drive-up in *Dude Where's My Car?*) Also, don't use this organization just because it's easy; a chronological order should be appropriate to what you plan to say.

✓ **Cause/effect:** If your research falls into this pattern ("first this happened, which caused that"), consider a cause/effect approach.

✓ **Problem/solution:** Another common order is to present a problem first, and then detail a solution to that problem.

✓ **Ranked by importance:** If there isn't a pattern to the data, you can arrange the ideas in ascending (or descending) order by importance.

✓ **In addition to putting the ideas into order, evaluate your material for each of the main points you want to make:** Do you have details, examples, evidence to back up your assertions? If not, you may need to go back and do some additional research.

Writing

You've brainstormed and have come up with a topic. You've done your research and arranged your ideas. Now it's time to face that blank page. Here's where most students freak, because they don't know what to say. Often, this leads to a paper in which the writer includes other people's thoughts strung together with a few connecting words. But that paper (and that writing method) is weak.

Readers = Writers

Good writers are good readers. When you read, you notice what makes a piece effective. You think about what details stand out and how the work is structured. Some writers may even mimic a certain author's writing style as they go through the process of finding their own unique voices.

Instead, you need to take your research and interpret in your own way. How do you do this? Start by quizzing yourself.

Ask yourself the typical journalism questions: who? what? when? where? why? how? Think about what makes the topic unique. Summarize why the topic is important.

Identify any tension or controversy about your topic. What are the main issues? What are the conflicting sides or the pros and cons? If there is controversy over the topic, decide on what the consensus is and then ask yourself, "Do I agree? Disagree?"

Think about how your topic relates to similar ideas. How does it fit within the overall big picture? Look into how your topic is structured or covered. Consider how your topic has changed or developed over time. Think about what your topic impacts or influences. Ask yourself whether things might have turned out differently for any reason and if so, what are the implications of a different turnout.

These queries should generate your own ideas on the content. You can then sit down and put pen to paper (or fingers to keyboard).

When you start writing, don't worry about being perfect in your first draft. Just get the words on the paper. Let it flow. Tell a story. Be yourself.

Editing

One of the common assumptions about writing a paper is that good writers can sit down and write a paper in one draft. Not true. Even the best writers revise their work, sometimes multiple times.

Read Twice

It's hard to complete both edits — editing for meaning and grammar — in the same reading. Instead, focus on one task at a time, doing two distinct reviews.

Please Check My Grammar

Most students want others to read their work to correct grammar, but that's your job. It's better to ask a friend or classmate to evaluate the content, the organization, and the ideas rather than review the grammar.

Editing your paper is what makes a so-so paper good or even excellent.

When you first start writing, you don't worry about being perfect. That's because you're going to come back and revise, edit, tweak, correct, elaborate, fix, and check your work. You'll do a detailed edit of the ideas, content, organization, and summary. In addition, you'll proofread your work, checking for spelling or grammatical errors. The following section covers some editing strategies and also provides a checklist for evaluating your work.

EDITING STRATEGIES

One way to review your paper is to read it aloud. Doing so can give you a good sense of the flow. You'll spot places where writing is choppy or where the transition from idea to idea is too abrupt.

As another strategy, ask a classmate or friend to read your paper. Have him or her pretend to take the other side and point out the weaknesses in your arguments.

Ask your instructor to read a draft. This is especially helpful if you're struggling with your paper. Your instructor may be able to ask a few questions to get you back on track or help you find research you need to beef up up your paper.

Consider your school's writing resources. Some schools have a writing center or writing tutors who can help with your writing. If so, these are good places for editing help.

TAKING ADVANTAGE OF YOUR WORD PROCESSING PROGRAM

It's common for students to use a computer and a word processing program such as Word to compose a paper. With its built-in tools, a word processor can check your spelling and grammar, allow you to view an outline, handle inserted illustrations, and help you make other editing changes. This short section gives you a few tips for writing with a word processing program.

Most programs flag misspellings and incorrect grammar. You can correct these on the fly or wait until the end, and then run a spelling and grammar check. Remember that this check isn't error-free; you still need to proofread your work.

Looking for the "right" word? Try looking up synonyms, using the program's thesaurus feature.

To rearrange text, you can use the Edit→Copy and Edit→Paste commands. One thing that's great about word processing programs is that you can usually undo changes. So if you accidentally delete text, you can even undo your deletion.

If you're using a word processing program, make sure you follow the specific style guidelines for the format of the assignment, such as the font size, margins, and so on.

REVIEWING AN EDITING CHECKLIST

When reading for content, consider the following:

✓ **Is the topic interesting?** Do you open with a strong statement?

✓ **Do you argue a unique point in the paper?** Make sure the paper isn't just a rehash of what others have said. Add your own unique ideas.

✓ **Do you have enough evidence to back up your assertions? Is any information missing?** Make sure that each point you make is well-supported with details. If needed, add any other information that is needed to prove your point or idea to your audience.

✓ **Have you included information that isn't relevant?** Some-times, you'll come across a fact or idea that's interesting, but that doesn't really pertain to your topic. Some students want to include all the information they find; after all, it took some work to gather that information. It's much better, though, to sift through and weed out any extraneous information — information that doesn't really relate to the topic.

✓ **Do you include the opposing view?** Many students ignore the other side's argument for controversial topics, but you shouldn't. Instead, acknowledge any opposing opinions. You can then counter those arguments, explaining why that reasoning is invalid or not applicable.

✓ **Do the ideas flow?** Are they arranged in a logical order? Do paragraphs transition from one idea to the next? Are the ideas balanced? Look at length of sentences and paragraphs. Your paper is lopsided if you cover one point in great detail (long paragraph) and the rest in short paragraphs.

✓ **Are all your sources cited?** Did you forget any sources? Most often instructors ask you to follow MLA guidelines for citing works. If you don't have this style guide book, you can find information on the Internet at www.mla.org.

✓ **Did you follow the instructor's style guidelines** for font styles and sizes, margins, the title page, headers or footers, and the bibliography or Works Cited page?

✓ **Did you check for errors?** Be sure to correct any spelling or grammatical errors. Also, don't rely on the grammar or spell checker in your word processing program; these aren't fool-proof, so you still need to proofread your work. If grammar isn't your strong point, find and use a good grammar guide-line book. You can spoil an otherwise perfect paper with sloppy grammar.

Finally, using your assignment as a guide, check that you've met all the requirements of the project.

The End

Is your writing over after the project has been turned in? Nope. When you get the paper back, take some time to review the grade and comments. What did you do well? What could you have done better? What did you learn from this assignment? Like any skill, writing improves with practice.

9

Using Technology

> *If you think of learning as a path, you can picture yourself walking beside her rather than either pushing or dragging or carrying her along.*
>
> —Polly Berrien Berends

Throughout this book, you've found information about how technology can improve your study habits, help you with research, and more. If you have a computer, you have lots of ways you can employ it in your school work. This chapter focuses on how you can get the most from your computer; it also provides some advice on how to organize your computer and work so that you don't lose key documents or aren't susceptible to computer viruses and other problems.

Even if you don't have a computer, you probably have access to one at your school, a library, or at a friend's house. If you don't have access, this chapter also includes ideas for accomplishing the same tasks without a computer.

Using a Computer for . . .

A computer is a handy tool for many school assignments. To that end, the following sections focus on some ways you can use a computer in your studies. These include using a computer for writing, doing research, communicating with other students, calculating numeric data, creating charts or graphs, taking digital pictures, shooting videos, and getting extra help.

WRITING

One of the most common ways people use a computer is as a replacement for the old-fashioned typewriter or pen and paper. Rather than type a paper or write out a paper long-hand, for example, you can use your computer and a word processing program, such as Word, to type it.

Using a word processing program for any kind of written work provides many benefits, including the following.

✓ **You can easily correct mistakes,** either as you type (using the Backspace or Delete key) or when you review your work.

✓ **You can reorganize the contents of the writing.** Sometimes, when you review your work, you find that one sentence or paragraph belongs before another. Or your conclusion may actually work better as an introduction. With a word processing program, you can easily move information to a different location. You can also delete sentences, paragraphs, and words (to get rid of repetition or to correct mistakes) and copy passages (if you want to use them again in the same or another document).

✓ **You can make formatting changes to improve the appearance of the document.** For example, in a research paper, you can make the section headings bold and bigger so that they stand out. You can emphasize new terms by italicizing them. You can create bulleted or numbered lists, add a border to a paragraph, change the page margins, create headers and footers, and more.

✓ **Check your spelling and grammar.** You can use the spelling checker to make sure your paper doesn't include any typographical errors. Most word processing programs also enable you to check your grammar. Note, however, that neither of these tools is foolproof. The spelling checker only flags words it can't find in its dictionary; it doesn't know whether you used each word correctly. (For example, the spelling checker won't flag "their" even if it should be "there.") The grammar checker also doesn't catch all errors and may flag sentences that are already correct. So, you still must proofread and correct your work.

✓ **Insert graphic elements.** You can also insert pictures, illustrations, graphs, charts, *clipart* (pre-drawn art), and other visual image files into your document.

✓ **Create outlines.** Most programs have an outline feature that helps you type up an outline, which is a great planning tool when writing papers or creating research assignments.

These are the key benefits of using a word processing program. As your assignments get more difficult, you may need to insert footnotes or endnotes or create a Table of Contents. Word processing programs can help create these and other elements.

Doing Research

Chapter 7 focuses on doing research and discusses how you can, with an Internet connection, look up facts, statistics, and other information. You can search for data on a topic for a research assignment. You can also browse through current news stories to find one suitable for a class discussion. You may search for more information on a topic. The "Tips for Doing Internet Research" section later in this chapter shares more information about how to search the Internet.

COMMUNICATING WITH YOUR INSTRUCTOR AND WITH OTHER STUDENTS

With an Internet connection, you can easily communicate with anyone who has an e-mail address. You can send e-mail messages to your instructor or to other students. You can also attach files to an e-mail message. For example, you can proactively e-mail an assignment to your instructor if you must miss a class. Your instructor may, in response, e-mail you what you've missed during your absence and tell you what homework you need to complete.

Most schools have Web sites, and some instructors are able to post important information on the site. For example, you may find a list of test dates, or you may find links for solving extra problems or handouts. Having a Web site not only lets you and the instructors stay in contact but also provides a way for students and parents to stay up-to-date on school activities.

Another way to communicate is by using Instant Messaging (IM). You set up a list of your *buddies* and their screen names. If one of these students is online when you are, you'll be notified. You can then send text messages to each other by typing and sending the message. This can be helpful if you want to ask a classmate for clarification about an assignment. You can also use Instant Messaging to talk to and make new friends online (within your school and beyond school). Keep in mind that you can easily get distracted by messaging. If you are studying, keep the messaging to a minimum or log off so that you can focus on your work.

CALCULATING NUMERIC DATA AND CREATING CHARTS

In some classes, you may be required to calculate and study numeric data beyond solving typical math problems. For example, in a practical math class like business math, you may have to track the income and expenses of a small company. To help store and create formulas for calculating data, you may use a *spread-sheet program* (for instance, Excel).

You use spreadsheet programs to create worksheets. A *worksheet* consists of a grid of rows and columns, and the intersection of a row and column is a *cell*. You can enter text or numbers into the cells. You can then create formulas to perform calculations on your entries. For example, you may want to sum all of the products sold within the first quarter. Or you may want to determine the average price of a list of products and prices. You can use a spreadsheet program to create anywhere from simple to complex formulas, such as figuring out the payments on a loan or calculating amortization.

One of the benefits of using a spreadsheet program is that it accurately calculates results (unless you've made an incorrect entry or created the formula incorrectly). You can change any of the entries referenced in the formula, and the formula will be recalculated immediately, saving you plenty of time. You can also use a spreadsheet program to create a database list; the program also includes commands for working with lists of like data. For example, you could sort all customers in your sample company by state. You can add subtotals for each sales region to see the total of sales by region, as well as the grand total.

In fact, if you plan to venture into business management, sales and marketing, or some financial field, you'll most likely use a spreadsheet program, even if you aren't introduced to it in your classes.

Another tool found in spreadsheet programs is the ability to create a chart. A *chart* can show at a glance a trend or a key aspect of the data. For example, a pie chart of product sales can help you easily spot your best-selling product. Line charts can help you spot trends over time, such as whether sales are decreasing (and, if so, by how much) or increasing.

You can even use a chart to illustrate data from a science experiment, such as a range of temperatures over several weeks or the growth rate of plants. Or suppose that, as part of a math class, you have to create a fictional business and forecast sales; you can do so with a chart. While charts might not be appropriate for your current studies, you'll probably find that creating them is a useful tool in other classes as you further your education.

TAKING PICTURES OR CREATING VIDEOS

With the advent of digital cameras and digital video recorders, many students are familiar with how to take pictures and create movies using a digital camera. If not, you can still use the traditional methods for taking pictures and creating videos.

For research assignments, you can take pictures and insert them in your report. For example, you can document plant growth for a science project on the effects of using a fertilizer by taking photographs at various stages. Likewise, you can take pictures of something in nature to use in an art assignment.

Digital cameras offer several advantages over their non-digital counterparts. First, you can preview every picture (and delete and retake them, if needed). Second, you can get prints quickly, using your computer, a film printing kiosk, or traditional printing services. (You can also order prints online, but that takes longer.) Third, you can copy pictures from your camera to the computer, and then use photo-editing changes to make changes or repairs to each picture. For example, you can fix red-eye or crop the picture so that the focus is on a particular portion of the photo.

Digital video cameras have also become popular, which means you may be challenged to create a movie as part of a project. For example, you might create a film of a skit based on a novel you've read. You can create a film to demonstrate some activity, such as playing an instrument or performing an experiment.

If you don't have digital camera technology available to you, you can still find pictures (in printed works or online) to use in your research assignment. Also, rather than filming a skit, you can perform it in class. In the end, the creativity and applicability of your pictures or videos are what's most important, not the method you used to create them.

GETTING EXTRA HELP

Computers are also an excellent method to get extra help on a topic or subject that you find difficult. For example, if you're struggling with math, you can purchase a practice math program with a CD that includes sample problems (and answers). In fact, your textbook or course materials may include a CD component for extra studies. You can also purchase a program to help you study a foreign language, such as Spanish or French, and use this program to practice at home.

You'll find that you can purchase educational software on a variety of topics and subjects. Look for these programs at discount stores (such as Target, Wal-Mart, Kmart, Sam's, or Costco), at electronic and computer stores (like Best Buy, Circuit City, or CompUSA), and at office supply stores (like Office Depot, OfficeMax, or Staples), and online.

You may also be able to find free help online. For example, you can find sites that help with vocabulary or explain science in terms that may be easier for you to understand. See the "Searching the Internet Using a Search Tool" section later in this chapter for tips on searching the Internet.

If you don't have a computer, you can also find print resources to help with the same tasks. For example, you can find printed workbooks for practicing algebra, grammar, spelling, reading and comprehension, and other topics.

Before Purchasing . . .

Before you purchase a software program as a tutorial, check your school or local library. Either or both may have resources that you can borrow.

Tips for Keeping Your Work Organized and Safe

Many students don't have a computer of their own, but share one with parents or siblings. Even if you do have your own computer, it's important that you keep it organized. Doing so helps you find what you need without wasting a lot of time. Being organized also helps you safeguard your data. The following sections focus on some guidelines for ensuring that you keep your computer work organized.

SAVING YOUR WORK

The most important skill you can learn when using a computer to create a document (a report, a letter, a worksheet, a picture — anything that you create using the computer) is to save your work. You should save and save often; otherwise you may lose important data. Imagine if you've just finished typing a six-page research assignment (and haven't saved), and your little brother unplugs the computer, there's a power outage, or your computer freezes up. All your hard work would be lost! Saving is critical. Therefore, keep these tips in mind when creating work on a computer.

✓ **Don't wait until you finish the document to save your work.** Save every five to ten minutes or, perhaps, even more often, and always after finishing a major part or change. Also save your work before you attempt something that you're not sure is going to turn out (such as formatting the document differently).

✓ **The first time you save a document, specify a logical location (a drive and folder) and a file name.** Save the document in a folder where similar documents are saved; you find out more about folders in the following section. Use a descriptive name that reminds you of the content of the document. If you name a document something generic like Homework1 or LitQuestions, you won't be able to tell exactly what these documents contain. Use something more descriptive, such as Lesson 3 Biology Homework or Lit Questions Huck Finn.

✓ **In addition to saving, consider making a backup copy of your work.** For example, suppose you're working on a series of short stories. Rather than just save them on the computer's hard drive, make a backup copy to a disk, keychain drive, or a CD, and then store the extra copy someplace safe. This ensures that if anything happens to the original, you can always use the backup copy. (Be sure to update your backup copy as you make changes to the original.)

✓ **If you work on a project at school (or at home, and then take it to school), save the document to a disk or keychain drive.** Note that it's a good idea to save or copy the document from the disk or keychain drive to the hard drive and work from the hard drive. When you're finished, you can then copy the updated document back to the disk or keychain drive, if needed. This way, if you copy the document to the hard drive, you'll have an extra copy — the disk or keychain drive version and the hard drive version.

CREATING AND USING FOLDERS

When you use a computer, especially if you share that computer with someone else, you want to keep your work stored in an organized way. Just as you probably keep physical folders or notebooks for each subject, consider setting up storing bins (called *folders*) for your work saved on a computer. If you just use the computer to type papers, set up a folder for these papers that's named something like "Josie's Papers." If you use the computer to create many different types of documents, you may want to create other folders. For example, you might have a folder for "Skylar's Pictures" or "Brendan's Music."

You can create folders based on the type of items they include or by project. For example, create a folder named "Science Project" to store all the different files you create for a science project (photographs, charts, reports, and so on).

As another option, you can set up folders for each person that uses the computer. You'll then have a dedicated folder for your work. If you have just a few files, this one folder might work. If not, create folders within your main folder for the different types of documents or projects. Or use some other organizational method to keep similar documents stored together.

You can use Windows (the operating system of most computers) to create folders. Use the Help and Support command to find out how to create a folder on your particular computer. (If you have a Mac, your operating system is called SystemX, where "X" is a version number or name. Use Help to figure out how to create a folder on your Mac if you don't know how.)

Printing Your Work

Most often, you create a document to print and share it with others (instructor and classmates, for example). You may also print a copy of a document so that you can proofread and correct any errors before turning in your final version. Finally, you may print a document to save a hard copy in your files.

Moving Documents

When you save a document, you can specify the folder in which to save it. If you accidentally save a document to the incorrect folder, you can move it to the correct folder. Check your particular operating system for help on how to move a file from one folder to another.

Preview the Document

Many programs enable you to preview a document before you print. Do this to avoid wasting paper. You can determine whether the pages look as you intend and correct any mistakes before you print.

Printing is straightforward: you usually select File→Print, and then click OK or Print to print the document. You also can specify print options, such as the quantity and range of pages to print. Check with your specific printer and program for information on printing your work.

Tips for Doing Internet Research

Chapter 7 focuses on the Internet as one possible resource for research; this section goes into more detail about using the Internet, including how to search the Internet, how to note favorite sites, and how to protect your computer from outside intruders, which is a potential threat when you use your computer to connect to the Internet.

SEARCHING THE INTERNET USING A SEARCH TOOL

When you're researching a topic using the Internet, the most common way to see what's available is to search for that topic. You can use any number of search tools for your search. In fact, your home page (the page you see when you log on to the Internet) may include a tool for searching. You can also go to sites specifically

Go to a Site

To go directly to a site (whether a search site or a site you want to visit), type the address to that site in the Address box, and then press Enter.

designed for searching. Some popular sites include Yahoo! (www.yahoo.com), Google (www.google.com), Ask Jeeves (www. askjeeves.com), Alta Vista (www.altavista.com), and others.

Some sites, such as Yahoo!, enable you to both do a general search and browse by category. For example, if you're doing a health report, you can click the Health link, and then review relevant stories, links, images, and other information on this topic. You can also search for a specific topic using the Search the Web text box. Other sites, in particular Google, have plain starting pages (but are still powerful search tools).

The basics for searching vary a little from site to site, but most follow the same process:

1. **Go to the search page.**
2. **Type the word or phrase you want to find.**
3. **Click the Search button.** The button will be named differently.
4. **Review the results of your search.**
5. **Click any of the search results to go to that site.**

The results are displayed differently depending on the search tool, but most contain similar information including the following:

✓ **Number of matches:** You should see an indicator of how many matches your entry matched, and it's often a very large number. You can scroll to the bottom of the page, where you'll see a link or page numbers that you can click to see the next page of matches.

✓ **Relevancy:** Different search tools determine which sites are more likely to be what you are looking for (their *relevancy*). These sites are often listed first. You may also see sponsored links along the side or at the top of the screen. Note that these sites have usually paid a fee to appear at the top of the page or along the side; that means they may not be the best matches.

✓ **Site description:** You should see the title of the page, its Web site address, and a brief description. Reviewing this information can usually give you a good idea of whether the site is relevant.

✓ **Search options:** If you get a lot of matches (and this is common), you may need to narrow the results to something closer to what you seek. Most search tools provide advanced search options that enable you refine the search. For example, you can specify words that you don't want included in the search, as one example. You can specify that the search results include all of the words you type in a phrase together. For example, if you type "White House," your list includes sites that include both "white" and "house." You can change the search so that only sites with "White House" together are listed.

Try Different Tools

If you search with one tool and don't find what you're looking for, try using a different search tool. Every tool will find and display different links.

Think Unique

When searching, try to think of a unique word or phrase as the search entry. And be as specific as possible. For example, if you're searching for the spotted owl, enter "spotted owl" rather than just "owl." If you're searching for information on a specific battle of Napoleon's, search for "Waterloo" rather than "Napoleon" or "Napoleon's battles."

SEARCHING FOR SOMETHING AT A PARTICULAR SITE

Many sites are composed of a number of pages. You not only have to find the site, but also where on the site the information you need resides. You have several options for locating a particular topic at a Web site.

Large sites usually include a tool you can use to search the site, so look for a Search This Site text box. (The name will vary.) If the site includes this tool, use it to search the site. The steps are similar to searching the Internet: Type the word or phrase, and then click the search button.

If the site doesn't include a search facility, it may have a site map; this shows what pages are included in the site and how they're arranged. You may be able to find the content you seek by checking out the site map.

As another option, you can use the search command in your Web *browser* (Web access software, such as Internet Explorer or Netscape Navigator) to search the site. In Internet Explorer, you can use the Edit→Find (on this Page) command to search the page for the word or phrase you seek.

KEEPING A LIST OF FAVORITE SITES

If you frequently use the Internet, you may find that some sites are useful for a variety of reasons (versus a site that served a single purpose for you and that you aren't likely to return to). To help you remember these sites, you can set up a list of favorite sites. Suppose you find a great reference site for looking up facts — you can add it to your favorites list. Rather than retyping the address to go to that site each time you want to visit, you can display your favorites list and select the site from the list.

In Internet Explorer, you add a site to your favorites list by first displaying the site and then using the Favorites→Add to Favorites command. To go to a favorite site, click the Favorites button to display your list of favorites in a pane along the left of the window. You then click a site in this list to quickly go to that site. (Different browsers use different terms. For example, Netscape calls this list Bookmarks.)

PROTECTING YOURSELF AND YOUR COMPUTER

When you use a computer, you need to take precautions to safeguard both your computer and your work from outside intruders. You can find entire books on this topic, as well as software packages designed specifically for this purpose. The following list just gives you an idea of the types of protection you should consider when using a computer online.

✓ **Protect against viruses.** A virus is a program that's spread through receiving e-mail messages, downloading programs, or sharing documents using a disk or keychain drive. Some

---

Organize Your List

If your list includes many sites, you can organize them into folders. For example, you may have a folder for your favorite music sites and another for writing reference sites (style guides, online dictionaries, and so on). You may have one that contains useful science information. Nearly all browsers enable you to add new folders when you add a site to the favorites list. Then, when you add a site to your list, you can select the folder. You can also organize favorite sites already on the list into different folders.

viruses are nuisances; they just display a silly message. Others can wreak havoc on your system, destroying files and even erasing all the information on your computer. To protect against viruses, use a virus protection program. This program scans e-mail attachments, files on disks and external drives, and your hard drive for viruses, and then fixes them when possible.

✓ **Avoid annoying intrusions when online.** Advertisers see the Internet as another avenue for advertising, and as such, you may be bombarded with *pop-up (or pop-under) ads;* that is, windows that open when you visit a Web site. You can purchase software to block these unwanted ads, and you may be able to download them for free from your Internet Service Provider.

✓ **Keep spies from spying on you.** Another annoying problem is spyware which is software that's installed on your system, usually without your knowledge. A spyware program tracks where you go online, and then relays this information back to its home site. Like viruses and pop-up ads, you can find (often free) software to remove and block spyware programs on your computer.

✓ **Keep out junk mail.** Yet another problem is junk e-mail (called *spam*). You may receive offers for all kinds of services and products (some quite embarrassing!). You can also block unwanted mail by blocking certain senders (those that send spam). You can also purchase programs to deal with spam, setting up rules that check for and flag suspected spam.

✓ **Protect your always-on Internet connection.** If you have a 24/7 connection, usually with a cable modem or DSL, your computer is always connected, which is convenient because you don't have to dial up each time you want to access the Internet. Without proper precautions, though, your computer may be open for intrusion by others. To protect your computer, you need to install special software (or hardware). The most common way to prevent unwanted intrusion is to set up a firewall.

Suites of Security and Privacy Programs

Security and privacy have become a major issue with the Internet. You can find programs that deal with a specific problem (such as spyware), as well as collections or suites of programs that bundle several privacy and security tools into one program. Norton Internet Security, for example, includes an anti-virus program, firewall protection, and spam features.

If you have your own computer, be sure to protect it from invasions. If your computer is shared by others, be sure someone is responsible for handling these issues. Your school and library should take the same precautions.

✓ **If you communicate with people you don't know online (in e-mail, in chats, or through Instant Messaging), be careful.** Never give out your real name, school, address, or any other identifying information about you unless you *know* that person. Also, never agree to meet someone you don't know in person, no matter what they promise you or how friendly or nice they seem online. Some criminal adults masquerade as teenagers to gain the confidence of kids. Err on the side of caution and don't give out personal details.

10

Getting Extra Help

> *In the middle of difficulty lies opportunity.*
>
> —Albert Einstein

Almost every student at one time or another struggles with a class or an instructor or just has a particularly rough time in his or her life. Before a problem escalates and grades deteriorate, you can avert disaster by getting help. Keep in mind that there's no shame in getting help from an instructor, a student teacher, an outside tutor, a book, or a software tutoring package that helps you get a handle on a difficult subject.

This chapter focuses on how to identify when you may need help, explains how to set up a good plan for tutoring, and describes the various tutoring methods from which you can select.

Deciding Whether You Need Help

During your school career, you may have times when you need extra help. The first steps in getting help are recognizing that you do need help, seeing what subject you're having problems with, and establishing the best plan to get you back on track in your studies.

Students are sometimes ashamed to admit that they're struggling, or they may feel they'll get in trouble if their grades drop

163

(especially if they have done well in the past). With this in mind, look for clues that a problem may exist at school in general, in a particular class, with a particular instructor, or with a certain student or group of students. Consider the following clues about potential problems:

✓ **Your grades drop.** If you've done well in the past, but your grades have dropped, it may mean that you're struggling with new content. For example, perhaps you always did well in math, but you're now having trouble understanding trigonometry.

✓ **You reach a plateau.** You may not be doing worse than before, but you aren't improving. In this case, a tutor, book, or other tool may be able to help you come up with strategies to re-energize your learning.

✓ **You just aren't interested in class.** This may be because you're bored and need to be in a more challenging class. And if you're not underchallenged, the class or instructor may just be boring! Even so, you need to look for some element of the topic that interests you. Think about the topic in a broad way, seeing how it relates to subjects you are interested in. See whether you can tie in ideas and topics that you do find of interest to your boring class. In addition, tutoring may be able to help you deal with frustration with a topic that's giving you fits.

No Good!

It's easy to say "I'm just not good at . . ." when you struggle in a particular topic. But this attitude doesn't serve you well as you continue your school career. Yes, you may find that some subjects are harder to understand, but that doesn't mean that you're doomed — that you won't ever be able to understand that topic, or that you can't improve. In fact, that's the purpose of getting help: spending extra time, trying different approaches, and making an effort to do better.

✓ **You've stopped doing homework and don't turn in other assignments.** This may indicate a struggle with your class or other problems, like too many parties, friends who aren't serious about studying, or instructors with whom you don't click. School performance, especially a drop in performance or interest, can indicate more than just problems with the academic and learning. If this sounds like you, talk to someone you can trust — a friend, an instructor, a counselor, or your parents.

✓ **You're trying your best, but you just can't grasp the concepts in a class.** Students learn using a variety of methods, and most students have a preferred learning style. Some students learn best visually, while others learn best by doing. A different approach, possibly with a tutor, can help you tackle a subject using a different learning style and make learning easier for you.

Now that you know some of the signs that indicate problems on the horizon, you can best decide how to handle them, first by identifying that there is a problem, and then by recognizing that you can use extra help.

IDENTIFYING THE PROBLEM

To identify a possible problem, seek input from instructors and parents. (Yes, your parents should also be allowed to contribute their input!) Also ask yourself the following questions:

✓ **Are you doing your work?** If not, why not? Is it a time management problem — that is, you are just not putting the effort into doing the work? Or are you frustrated because you don't understand how to complete the work? In the first case, consult with a book on time-management to get advice on how to schedule your time. (Chapter 2 contains some basic advice on time-management.) You may find that you need to cut back on social and extracurricular activities in order to give yourself more time. Or you may need to structure your study time differently. In the second case, that you're frustrated by your assignments, you may benefit from the help of a tutor.

(Tutoring is covered in the "Getting Outside Tutoring" section later in this chapter.)

✓ **Are you attending class?** Are you overloaded and don't have time to attend every class? Or are you skipping class because the work isn't done, because you feel stupid, or because you're bored? Think about what would make you want to go to class. Talk to your instructor, advisor, and/or counselor for ideas.

✓ **Why do you think you're struggling?** Is there too much material covered too quickly? Are there distractions in class? Are other classmates struggling? Answering these questions helps pinpoint the problem area. If the speed of the class is overwhelming, a tutor may be able to help you keep up with the tempo so that you can better grasp the subject and keep up. If other students are struggling, that may be a sign that the instructor needs to adapt the timing or amount of work. Also, if there are distractions (such as discipline problems with other students), you may need to mention these to the instructor or to a counselor or advisor.

✓ **Do you understand the material but have problems with tests?** If so, a tutor may be able to help you learn the best methods for studying for tests. Chapters 4 and 5 include strategies for studying for tests.

✓ **Do you have a problem with the instructor?** Everyone at one time or another runs into an instructor with whom they have a conflict. As a student, always remain respectful, but if you think you're being singled out or treated unfairly, consider talking with the instructor to see whether there has been some misunderstanding. Ask the instructor what you can do to succeed in class; doing so shows your willingness to work. If that doesn't work, note any clear examples of bias, and then present this information to your counselor or advisor. You can then decide how to best approach the situation, working with the instructor and school administrators. (Sometimes it's just a misunderstanding or preconceived idea — perhaps the instructor heard something you said about the class and took it out of context.) Addressing the problem head on, honestly and respectfully, is usually the best way to handle the situation.

✓ **Finally, and most importantly, do you think you need help?** Tutoring isn't going to help unless you buy into the idea of tutoring.

CREATING A PLAN FOR IMPROVEMENT

After you've identified the need for extra help and you've identified the problem, you can create a plan for how to help improve your performance.

As a student, think about what would help you do better in class. Do you need more time to do your work? Do you need someone to explain things differently and at a different pace? Do you need help reading and understanding the information?

Make a list of what would help you do your best in class. Then, working with your instructor and guidance counselor or advisor (and, potentially, your parents, depending on your age and level in school), see whether they agree with your list. You may need to make some compromises. Your instructor, for example, may have insight into what can help you learn more easily. Because he or she likely has a lot of experience, do consider any suggestions. Your counselor/advisor or parent may recognize other situations (such as a part-time job or too many social or extracurricular activities) that need to change.

When you, your instructor, counselor or advisor, and (perhaps) your parents have agreed on the best approach, you can consider the various resources available for improving your performance, as described throughout the rest of this chapter.

Working with School Resources

Start at the school and look into the resources that are offered. Does your school have counseling? Special tutors (besides the instructors)? Reading aides? Resources to handle attention deficit disorder (ADD) or attention deficit hyperactivity disorder (ADHD)? Look first for these resources (which are usually free and easy to access), and then consider outside resources.

Your school is a good place to start, because the professionals there know your strengths and weaknesses. They see you day after day in class and have a good sense of not only how you work but also how you work best. They may also have insight into what causes some of your struggles (perhaps a lack of class participation, not asking questions when you don't understand, slower reading, difficulty expressing your thoughts in writing, and so on). Second, they know the curriculum; that is, they know what subjects you need to master and at what level.

HAVING YOUR INSTRUCTOR (OR INSTRUCTOR AIDE) TUTOR YOU

Sometimes, an instructor can provide after-school tutoring, giving you one-on-one attention. You can make arrangements with the instructor on the time, the length of tutoring required, as well as compensation (if any) for the tutoring. You and your instructor should come up with predetermined goals and ways to measure those goals so that you can monitor the success of the tutoring.

If an instructor isn't available, your class may have an instructor's assistant. Depending on this person's role and background, he or she may be available for tutoring. Again, you'd need to decide on the goal, the scheduling, the way to measure progress, and the compensation (if any).

Never-ending Tutoring

One thing that students can worry about is that once tutoring starts, they'll be tutored forever. At the first session, set up a timeline with definite dates about the start and end of the tutoring.

Checking In

Be sure to evaluate the tutoring. Is it helpful? A waste of time? Should something be changed? Is the time frame right? (You may meet daily, twice a week, weekly, or on some other schedule.) Do you need to meet more often? Less often?

WORKING WITH A READING EXPERT

Some students struggle with reading and may have a learning disability such as attention deficit disorder (ADD). Because special reading requirements for ADD have become so prevalent, many schools employ reading experts who can help slow readers improve their reading skills. These specialists can also help students with reading disabilities come up with strategies or techniques to deal with their situations or special needs.

WORKING WITH A STUDENT TUTOR

Another tutoring option is working with a student tutor. Some students feel more comfortable working with a peer, and it's also a good experience for the student tutor to help classmates. The student tutor may or may not be in the same grade, but will have experience in tutoring. For example, students who are good in math may participate as math tutors at all levels. Students who are good writers can help other students with their written assignments.

Like working with an instructor tutor, you should set goals with a student tutor, set up a schedule for the tutoring sessions, decide on compensation (which may be determined by the school — for example, some students get service hours for tutoring in lieu of payment), and decide how to determine whether the tutoring is successful.

No Reading Specialist?

If your school doesn't have a reading specialist on staff, ask for recommendations. Because this is a fairly common problem, most schools should have referrals for you to consider.

Getting Outside Tutoring

If the school resources don't seem to be working or if you don't feel comfortable in that tutoring situation, you can seek outside help. An outside opinion can provide new insight and solutions to problems. In addition to hiring a tutor not associated with school, you can also use the services of tutoring centers, check into books, or use CD-based and Web-based tutoring courses. Another option, especially if you feel as though you're falling behind your grade level, is to take courses in the summer.

The following sections discuss some outside tutoring resources to consider.

HIRING A TUTOR

If your school doesn't provide tutoring at the level or in the subject you need, or if you don't feel comfortable working with a tutor at school, you can hire an outside tutor to help with your work. This situation works similarly to working with an instructor tutor; that is, you determine your goals, set up a regular meeting schedule, decide how to measure progress, and communicate with the tutor and your instructor as to how the tutoring is working.

To find a tutor, ask for recommendations either from your school or from friends or families who have used outside tutoring resources. If you can't come up with any recommendations, you can look up tutoring services on the Internet or in the Yellow Pages. In either case, prepare a list of questions. Some possible questions include:

✓ How long have you been tutoring?

✓ How many students do you tutor each week?

✓ What are your teaching experiences?

✓ Do you hold an instructor certification or an advanced degree?

✓ Do you specialize in a certain area?

✓ How much do you charge?

Get references from the tutor and call those references to get a firsthand account of how the tutoring session worked for them. You might ask questions of these references such as:

✓ Was the tutor timely and responsible?

✓ Did you show improvement?

✓ What activities did the tutor use to teach you?

✓ What is your opinion of the tutor?

TUTORING CENTERS

In addition to tutors, you can also find tutoring centers that hire many tutors with many areas of expertise. At a tutoring center, you can engage in one-on-one tutoring sessions as well as set up group tutoring. Like finding an independent tutor, ask for recommendations. If you find one through the Yellow Pages or Internet, diligently check out the company's background and qualifications.

Tutoring Does Not Equal Dummies

Tutoring is not a sign that you lack intelligence. Students at all levels seek tutoring. Some are great students in most subjects but struggle in one. Others take advanced classes because they're planning ahead for college and use tutoring to help them gain an academic advantage. All want to improve their performance.

Using Other Tutoring Resources

Not all students like to work with a tutor. Perhaps they are shy or feel intimidated if they don't know the right answers. If you're one of these students, you may like tutoring resources that you can do on your own. These may include books, workbooks, CD-based training, Web courses, and so on. Ask your school for recommendations or visit an educational supply store. You'll even find that popular retail stores (like Target or Wal-Mart) and bookstores of all sizes sell these types of resources.

Often, the publisher makes the learning entertaining and fun rather than just listing a bunch of problems and answers. These guides can engage you and help you progress at your own pace. For example, I had a student who struggled with fractions, so I bought him a small fraction workbook. After he worked through that, he gained confidence, and his grades improved. Workbooks and other self-paced resources help you practice skills on your own time that you may not have time to practice during school.

Also note that these guides aren't just for students that struggle. Often the best students use study guides as a way to practice, and the grades they get are a reflection of the work they put into studying.

Taking Summer Courses

Another option is to take summer courses, workshops, or seminars. This may be helpful in the following cases:

- ✓ If you failed a course or didn't do well, consider taking a summer course so that you don't fall behind the rest of your class.

- ✓ If you passed a class but really didn't understand it and that class will be the basis for classes in the next school year, you may want to take a summer course.

- ✓ If your progress as a student is fine but you want to improve in a particular area, you might take a summer course. For example, if you want to learn to be a better writer, you might take a summer creative writing class or workshop.

✓ If you're planning on going to college, you may want to take some college-credit courses so that you start off a little ahead when you do go to college.

✓ If you're interested in a subject, but it's not offered at your school or you can't fit it in your schedule, you may take a workshop, seminar, or class on that subject at a local community center or college. For example, you may take a drama workshop or an art class. Or you might take organic chemistry, because it's not offered at your school. You may be able to take these as credits that apply toward your diploma or degree, or you might just take them for fun (and not worry about the grade you receive).

Index